Borderline Personality Disorder Survival Guide for You and Your Relationship

Manage, Treat and Recover BPD Through the Power of Dialectical Behavioral Therapy

Julie Griffiths

herein.

Additionally, the information in the following pages is intended only for informational purposes and should thus be thought of as universal. As befitting its nature, it is presented without assurance regarding its prolonged validity or interim quality. Trademarks that are mentioned are done without written consent and can in no way be considered an endorsement from the trademark holder.

Table of Contents

Introduction

Congratulations on taking the first big step toward improving your life! Whether you are suffering from Borderline Personality Disorder or have someone in your life who is, it can be a struggle with seemingly no end in sight. But there is hope!

Just your willingness to look at ways to improve your life and your relationships says a lot for your ability to actually do so. It takes that first step, and here you are now, taking it!

The Borderline Personality Disorder Survival Guide will keep you going with a wealth of information and steps you can take to keep you going on your path toward improving your relationships, and improving how you view yourself. Come back to it time and time again to reinforce the information, and bring positive change into your life.

By starting to learn more about BPD and how you can cope and manage your emotions, you can take back control of your life. Here you are making an important first step. There are many available options out there, some better than others. Everyone who struggles with BPD does so in a different way. You are *not* alone.

Learning, educating yourself, and finding new ways of coping are amazing steps to creating a healthier you! So, look within these pages, and find something you can use. The struggle with BPD is a lifetime, and it takes commitment to move forward. Congratulations on being someone who wants to better their life for you and your loved ones!

Chapter 1: What is BPD?

Borderline Personality Disorder (BPD) is a serious mental illness that can have devastating effects on the individual and those around them. It is an illness that needs treatment, which at one time was thought to be impossible. New studies have shown that there is a way that treatment can help, which is great news for those who suffer from the trauma induced by this illness.

Up to 5% of the population suffers from this illness. That is no small number on either side of the equation range. Most often, it is on young adults and teens where the diagnosis is first made. As high as 40% of young people in mental health institutions are suffering from BPD. But this is not an illness only experienced by the young. Many adults are finding that they are BPD sufferers as well.

However, it is worth noting that there are instances where the older the individual gets, more and more of the behaviors and symptoms that categorize and point to BPD start to slip away; they become less intense, making it easier to handle on some levels. The developing hormones of youth may have a part to play in that, and as the hormones stabilize through the adult years, so do the erratic emotions that come with hormonal changes.

This is not always the case, and it also doesn't help those younger people, even adults in earlier years, to deal with what they are facing each and every day of their lives *right now*.

Some of the traumatic experiences brought to the surface by BPD are symptoms shared with other mental illnesses, so sometimes it can be hard to get a handle on a diagnosis. Anti-social behavior, narcissistic personality traits, histrionic tendencies…

These are only a few of the traits of Borderline Personality Disorder that share symptoms with other mental illnesses such as anxiety disorders, schizophrenia, or one that is often commonly mistaken for BPD… Bipolar Disorder.

But there is a difference between these mental illnesses and BPD. It's not only in the symptoms but also in the way you feel and look at yourself and others. To fully understand BPD, let's begin by taking a look at what signs and symptoms are used to define and diagnose BPD, and then we can go from there.

Symptoms of BPD

There is a bundle of signs that are traditionally attributed to Borderline Personality Disorder. The most common defining trait of BPD is…

Fear of Abandonment

Those who suffer fear of abandonment have often had some form of traumatic childhood experience. When going through this at a young age, we are not given the coping tools to understand what is happening. An emotional reaction is formed and becomes the normal state of being—one of fear, loss, and stress. This carries through into our adulthood, giving us a lifetime of misunderstanding our own emotions, as well as not being able to properly read the emotional queues from others. Our ability to empathize with how others might be feeling is impaired. This leads to heightened fear and stress levels as we try to understand what others are feeling based on our own limited perspective.

Whether real or imagined, the fear of abandonment feels very real to those with BPD. It is one of the strongest and most prominent signs that indicate the presence of BPD and is the driving force behind many of their erratic emotional behaviors. Those with BPD will do anything they can to keep someone in their lives. The downside to this is that the very efforts they make, good or bad, can actually lead to pushing those away that they already fear will abandon them, creating a self-perpetuating, never-ending cycle.

But it doesn't have to be a never-ending cycle. Those with BPD, or the loved ones who understand the nature of their partners' emotional volatility can help work to break the cycle. There is hope! But it isn't easy, and the work has to be put in.

So, what does fear of abandonment look like? It is all person dependent, of course.

Clinging tightly to another person is a very common sign. Smothering them, hoping that by showing them that they are needed and necessary in their lives by living every moment they can around them and displaying themselves as weak to their partner's strength. Berating their partner when they are not around or haven't been around, to try and make them come around or be around even more.

Over texting is a sign of clinginess. The need to be aware of where their partner is every moment of every day. Making sure that their partner is aware that they are still there every chance they get. Getting upset when there is no immediate response. These are all classic clingy behaviors, now made even more possible and possibly devastating to their relationships by the insertion of technology into every part of our waking days.

Added to the list is constantly checking their partner's social media pages to see whether they have posted anything new. Spending time after time looking at every picture they have of their partner. Showing up somewhere just because they think their partner is going to be there too, without having been invited to go. Hanging onto them physically every moment they are together. Spending time doing whatever their partner wants, even if they are bored out of their mind. Irrational jealousy and trying to speed up the relationship too fast or attach themselves to the relationship too quickly, even if the partner they are interested in is not available…

These are all signs of the clingy side of fear of abandonment.

What else does fear of abandonment look like?

Fear of abandonment can take the opposite side of clingy as well. People who experience fear of abandonment can tend to not want to commit themselves to a relationship, just so they won't be left feeling abandoned at some point in the future. They may have multiple partners that they see regularly so that there is always someone waiting for them, even if another one of their partners walks away. That way, they will never feel alone. However, once they do find themselves in a committed relationship, they will do everything they can, and put up with whatever happens, no matter how unhealthy, just so they won't be left alone. They may even engage in unwanted sexual behavior, just to maintain a feeling of connection.

People who fear abandonment are often very picky and will nitpick over every little thing. Being emotionally intimate is difficult, because of the fear of committing emotions to someone who will just walk away. This fear is very real for them because BPD sufferers tend to feel very insecure and unworthy of being around, or of having someone in their lives. They base their worth and value on someone actually staying in their lives, and then sadly, unwittingly sabotage the relationship and when their partner leaves, and they then feel justified in their feelings on not being worthy of love.

This doesn't just happen with romantic life partners, it also happens with friends and family, perhaps a little differently for each relationship in their lives. It makes for very unstable relationships. When someone with BPD feels that they are on good grounds with the other person to their relationship (whether partner, family, friend, etc.), things are all positive, the other person can do no wrong. When something happens to upset the person with BPD in the relationship, that other person can now do no right. It's an all or nothing fixation.

Just to be clear… this is not a right or wrong. It just is. Remember… someone suffering from BPD will often base their own self-value or worth in the other person being in their lives. By making them "all good," they are all good. If the other person does something to upset the person with BPD, up to and including walking away from the relationship, in order for the BPD sufferer to feel they have value left, the other person must now become "all bad". It is their way of being able to cope with abandonment or even perceived abandonment.

Unstable or Fluctuating Image of Self

Part of the reason that BPD sufferers base who they are and their value on their relationships with others is that they are unsure of how they identify with themselves alone. They can go from euphoric and excited about life to emptiness and depression in no time flat. They experience life by each moment, rather than as a whole.

Many BPD sufferers will go through life changes, often drastic ones, from one thing to the next. One relationship to the next, one home to the next, one job or career choice to the next, even their sexual identity can be changeable in their world from one moment to the next. They have trouble identifying with who they are, except in the moment, and even then, this self-identity is often filled with negative values of self-worth. They may not even be able to recognize where those feelings are coming from, only that they are there. Feelings of shame, not being good enough, not being good at all—some even perceiving themselves as "evil".

Impulsive and Harmful Behaviors

These negative feelings that BPD sufferers assign to themselves bring along with them destructive behaviors, mood changes, gambling, drugs, drinking, spending sprees, reckless driving, shoplifting… anything to give substance to the voices in their head, proving that those voices are right. It can also be a way for them to either numb the overwhelming feelings of emotions, such as with substance abuse (drugs, alcohol) or to help them feel something when they are feeling numb or emptiness.

Suicide or Self-Harming Behaviors

Suicide or suicidal thoughts are not uncommon for BPD sufferers. The tendency to self-harm raises the numbers even higher. Up to 75% of BPD sufferers have harmed themselves in one way or another at least once in their lives. It's not just the negative behaviors that were listed above, which can be considered a form of self-harming behaviors.

The type of self-harm that is being referred to here is actual causing of physical harm to themselves. This can be in the form of suicide, some attempt to end their lives. It can also take the form of cutting, sticking (or injecting), burning themselves with cigarettes, or a multitude of other ways to inflict harm upon themselves. Sadly, the number of BPD sufferers who take their lives can be as high as 10%.

Emotional and Mood Swings

Emotional volatility is another prevalent symptom of BPD. Things that many of us may not even have hit our radar, such as a classmate passing by without saying hello, can send someone who suffers from BPD into emotional overload. These erratic mood swings can often be short-lived, sometimes lasting no longer than a few minutes to a few hours, but they can last as long as a few days. It is not just with simple events, such as the example above, but their emotions tend to be unregulated, which can cause them to jump from zero to full-blown in moments. Often these emotional reactions are highly disproportionate to what caused/triggered them in the first place.

Chronic Feelings of Emptiness

The other side of the emotional equation for BPD sufferers is what they describe as feeling completely empty. Feeling empty is a hard thing for many people to explain, and yet so many people suffer from it for various reasons, not all mental health-related.

For most, it is described as a feeling of being disconnected, especially emotionally, from everything and everyone else around you. This absence of emotional connection is more than just not feeling anything. Some people suffering from feelings of emptiness describe very physical or tangible feelings when they speak of feeling "empty".

There are feelings that something may be missing, but not necessarily anything they can put a finger on. Some people may feel bored and apathetic, like nothing matters. Feelings of extreme tiredness and/or lethargy are common. It is like an emotional numbness has taken them over, and they don't know how to respond to life, or how to reengage themselves back into life again.

Some describe themselves as feeling absolutely nothing or feeling as though they are nobody. This can be a dangerous doorway into which the negative behavior patterns can develop, drugs, drinking, sex, food, etc. ...just to be able to feel *something*.

Sometimes these feelings of emptiness stem from the individual trying everything outside of themselves to keep others in their lives, or even to just keep a handle on their lives. When they do this, they tend to neglect to care for themselves, and may eventually lead to feelings of unworthiness which in turn leads to emptiness. It can all be connected in a very vicious, very lonely, empty feeling cycle.

Disproportionate Anger

Also described as explosive anger, it is not uncommon among BPD sufferers. Their anger usually has a trigger, something that sets it off, but the anger that comes out is often far over the top when examined to being proportionate to what the trigger was in the first place. This is usually pretty evident when their feelings of anger are directed outward, at others or situations or events outside themselves. But BPD sufferers experience a lot of that same disproportionate anger directed inwardly at themselves on a regular basis.

Dissociative Paranoia

Another symptom that some BPD sufferers have to live with is the feeling that they are not themselves, or of themselves. Different from the feelings of emptiness, or feeling as if they are nobody, the feelings of dissociation actually make them feel as though they are not connected to themselves, as opposed to not being connected to others or things outside of themselves. Some describe it as a feeling of "looking in" from the outside when they examine themselves.

Because of the disconnection of self, it makes it hard to connect with others either. It is hard for people who can't connect to trust themselves, let alone to trust others. It can create feelings of paranoia that seep in and taint everything they view, always wondering whether the other person has some ulterior motive for doing whatever it is that they are doing. Stress can be a major factor that triggers paranoia in BPD sufferers, and a small percent of those who are under tremendous amounts of stress can actually experience a psychotic break or psychotic episode as a result.

Looking for Signs

While the most commonly known symptoms attached to those with Borderline Personality Disorder are listed above, it can be a very difficult illness to diagnose. Not everyone has all of the symptoms, and not everyone experiences them to the same extreme, or even in the same way as others with the same affliction. There are times when BPD is referred to as "Surplus Disorder" because there are so many possible symptoms and many of those cross over into other realms of mental illness. Additionally, it can be further complicated when other mental illnesses exist alongside the BPD, changing the symptoms they exhibit.

Yet with so many people being diagnosed with this disorder, it has created a severe mental health crisis that needs to be addressed. Thanks to the leaps and bounds made in many of our sciences, the science of psychiatry being no exception, we now have ways that BPD sufferers can be helped, whereas that was not once possible, with our limited knowledge in the past.

If you are just looking for answers, and have yet to be diagnosed, or have been diagnosed and are not sure what to do next, self-help techniques having value aside, it is imperative with any illness or mental illness to seek professional assistance in finding your way back to a healthier you.

Chapter 2: What You Should Know About BPD

There is a lot to learn about Borderline Personality Disorder both for those who suffer from it and/or for those who have someone who struggles from BPD in their lives. It is not something that can be fully examined and explored within the pages of a single text. However, there is a start to discovering some of the possible and common symptoms attributed to BPD sufferers. Hopefully, enough of a start that it should make you feel better that you are not alone!

Let's take a further look into the realm of BPD and what it can mean for you and your loved one(s).

Causes

While trying to discover the reasons why Borderline Personality Disorder can happen, they have been unable as of yet to directly connect it to genetics. That is to say, they have not yet discovered a specific "gene" that says someone is going to have BPD, unlike some other mental illnesses such as Bipolar Disorder (often confused with Borderline Personality Disorder, but is not the same), Autism, ADHD (Attention Deficit Hyperactivity Disorder), Schizophrenia, and even Major Depression Disorder.

Genetics

That being said, they have found that BPD has a strong connection to hereditary links within families. There is a predisposition toward the development of BPD in those who have first-degree relatives (mother, father, sister, brother, etc.) who already suffer to some degree from

BPD. It does not mean that if there is someone in the family who does have BPD that you will develop it as well, only that there is a higher chance, and it doesn't hurt to be aware of that possibility.

This predisposition factor is almost five times higher when there is a hereditary connection already present. It should also be said that even with a hereditary link present, that BPD is often triggered by external traumatic life experience or stress factors, ones that usually occur in childhood.

Social/Environmental Factors

With or without the hereditary factor, it is often a traumatic incident or incidents, or other high-stress situations that occur in childhood that trigger the onset of Borderline Personality Disorder. These can be anything from separation from parents, parental neglect, or parental insensitivity to unstable family factors, including a parent or close family member with an alcohol or substance abuse issue, mental disorder, or others factors that include child abuse or molestation or rape occurrences. Emotional validation can also be a huge factor, one that is not often considered when it comes to speaking in terms of abuse. This occurs when a child (or anyone) experiences an emotion, a feeling about an event, person, etc. and is told over and over again that they have no right to feel that way, that they shouldn't feel that way… that they are being silly or acting out for nothing.

It should be noted that the development of BPD is very complex, and no one person or thing is really at fault, but rather it is a culmination of multiple factors.

Abnormalities of the Brain

While an actual gene has not been discovered for Borderline

Personality Disorder, there is a genetic factor that can come into play with its development. While there is not a gene that can specifically designate the presence of BPD, there is what scientists have come to call the serotonin gene, a gene that controls the regulation of serotonin in the brain, that may be at least linked to the presence of BPD.

Serotonin is responsible for transmitting signals to our bodies that regulate our moods. Low serotonin levels are directly linked to states of depression. When our serotonin levels are in balance, or at higher levels, they contribute to our feelings of well-being, and our ability to feel happiness. They help to regulate our social interactions, our ability for sleep, and even our sexual desires. While not an actual gene that scientists can point to and say, "Hey… this is why you have BPD…," there have found at least some correlation, and further investigation may yield some deeper understanding at some point in the future.

Another consideration is neurologically based. Our brains are separated into distinct areas, each controlling a different aspect of ourselves and our personalities, memories, etc. There are connections made between various parts of the brain that occur with every action or emotional perception we make on any given day. It has been discovered that in people with BPD, these connections are not made as strongly in those parts of their brains that control decision-making, judgment, and emotions. There have been actual physical differences noted in the emotional regulation centers of those who suffer from BPD. The expression and experience of emotions can trigger a larger volume of activity in those centers, than with those who do not have BPD.

Diagnosis

Once again, it is difficult to diagnose Borderline Personality Disorder. Even the common symptoms find overlap in other mental disorders. Added to that, even when a competent professional makes an attempt at diagnosis, BPD is often confused for Bipolar Disorder, also sometimes referred to as BPD. One of the big differences between them is that Bipolar Disorder is something that can be helped with medications, in addition to therapy.

Borderline Personality Disorder sufferers do not have that benefit, but they are not without hope. BPD doesn't need chemicals for treatment. It is something that can be worked on within the individual, with loved ones, and through therapy. Coping mechanisms can be put into place, which we will be showing later in this book. And, the biggest benefit… it can become better as we age.

Diagnosis for BPD is done through evaluation by a professional. It can include a detailed medical history, and discussion of past traumatic events, and a long questionnaire that can be issued on paper or sometimes orally. Some of the specific criteria that professionals pay attention to are as follows:

- A frantic concern and efforts to avoid abandonment, whether it is real or imagined.

- "Splitting" when it comes to relationships, define by periods of intense idealization followed by periods of intense devaluation of their partners, of which their relationships are continuously unstable, or multiple because they can't manage a stable relationship (adding to the feelings of abandonment).

- Impulsive behavior, especially that of the negative variety, in which at least two behavioral traits can be identified, and can include participation in multiple sex partners, unsafe or unwanted sex, gambling, alcohol or other substance abuse, binge eating, spending sprees, etc.

- Consistent feelings of being empty of emotions, feeling non-existent, or empty.

- Out of proportion emotional responses or erratic emotional states, usually triggered by something the individual perceives, that are fairly short-lived, often lasting only minutes or hours, but not usually longer than several days.

- Extreme images of self-identity, usually to the negative.

- Instances of self-harming or suicidal behavior.

- Dissociation from self, feeling as though they are not connected to themselves, perceiving events as taking place to someone else, or paranoid episodes that can include a sense of unreality of the events taking place around them.

Support

There are support groups available for almost every mental illness, and Borderline Personality Disorder is no exception. Look for local resources available whether you are suffering from BPD yourself, or you are in a relationship with someone with BPD. Relationships are not confined to being the partner or mate of someone with BPD, it can also include family members and friends.

Therapy is also recommended for those suffering from BPD, and/or those involved in a relationship with someone who has BPD.

There are a few additional ways that can be offered in ways of support and will be mentioned here, in addition, to be covered later in further depth.

If You Suffer From BPD…

Acceptance

Acceptance is the first key to becoming a healthier, happier you. There are two ways that you can look at acceptance in the case of Borderline Personality Disorder. The first is acceptance in the same way that we look at the stages of grief. Grief and bereavement are not only relegated to the death or loss of someone outside of yourself. It can also be applied to those things you feel death or loss of as relates to yourself and your experiences. In this case, we are talking about BPD.

When we receive a diagnosis like BPD, it is a life-changing bit of information put into our hands. It is natural to go through the stages of grief in this case… Denial, Anger, Bargaining, Depression… We are in denial because we don't want it to be true. We get angry, because we think, "Why is this happening to me? I don't deserve this!" We bargain because we think that maybe there might be something that can just magically "make it go away." We get depressed because we know it won't just go away. Which leads us to the final point of acceptance.

For many, when hitting a place where they feel they have lost themselves, that this "diagnosis" they just received means they are no longer who they thought they were before they can reach true, healthy acceptance, they go through the gambit of the stages of grief. If they can't process at one stage or another, they can't move forward into a place of acceptance. There is a term for this in the psychiatric communities… bereavement disorder.

Acceptance of a BPD diagnosis doesn't mean that you don't

grieve for the loss of your sense of self. It doesn't mean that you make excuses for what happened to make it not your fault. It is *not* your fault. There is no *fault* here at all. It is something that happened to you and is still happening to you. Acceptance is realizing and recognizing that something is happening with you, and stopping the denial that it really is happening. With this acceptance, you are in a stronger place than you were because now you know what is going on, and you can actually take steps to move forward and do something about it to make yourself, your life, and those around you happier and healthier.

How do you cope with this kind of acceptance for the loss of your sense of self? If you are not ready, take your time and process it slowly, as you feel more ready. Don't put pressure on yourself to put it all behind you. You're not expected to just get over it. You may be able to work through the process of acceptance very quickly. You may need time for it to process. It doesn't matter. Do it in your own time. If you struggle with getting to the stage of acceptance, then reach out and ask for help, support, and understanding.

The second is a relief! All of these things that you have been experiencing actually have a name, and solutions for bringing you to a healthier state of living.

Avoid Drugs & Alcohol

This should go without saying, but it's being said anyway. Use of drugs and/or alcohol cannot only lead to self-harming behaviors, but they can also interact negatively with other medications that you are taking and can heighten and turn around your emotions, which is usually already a big concern for those diagnosed with BPD. Addiction centers are also heightened for those who have BPD. If you do imbibe in alcohol, monitor your intake, and be aware of how your mood may be altered. When dealing with BPD, emotional responses can already be out of proportion to the situation. Alcohol can make them even more, so it is highly recommended that alcohol and drugs are avoided, especially in the stages of working on yourself. Always be aware and be mindful of your emotional state.

Connect with Others

Not only is support offered in the form of groups, but there are additional means of connecting to other people who are going through the same things that you are. There are online groups and peer-to-peer chatrooms available for those who suffer from BPD. You can connect with others and find that not only are you *not* alone in what you are experiencing, but you can help each other find different ways of coping with different situations that arise.

Take Care of Yourself and Your Body

Negative self-identity is just one thing that can be helped when we stop to take the time to take care of ourselves. There are other things that can have a negative impact as well, such as certain foods or lack of exercise. Everything we do impacts every other part of our lives, and what we do or don't do to our bodies can impact us greatly. Not only will paying attention to how you are treating yourself, but exercise, especially something along the lines of Yoga or Tai Chi, can have beneficial calming effects to help better stabilize emotions.

Other methods can be effective too. Self-care is about protecting your own happiness and states of well-being. This is particularly necessary for those with BPD in times of stress. When you feel stress levels rising, or even if you just need to re-center and refocus, take a few minutes and focus on nothing but you!

Self-care techniques can be person or situational dependent. Try some or all of them and see what works for you.

Listen to Music. Music is a universal language, and it is a language that speaks "mood." Find a suitable playlist on Spotify or Youtube and listen to songs that evoke the mood you want to achieve, whether that is happy, nostalgic, upbeat, or calming, find what suits you and spend some time immersing yourself in a different emotion than what you are feeling.

Get Your Blood Moving, Focus on Your Breathing. The reason why Tai Chi and Yoga were mentioned above, is because they both incorporate both of these methods. If you are not feeling the urge, or don't have the time to sit down with a Tai Chi or Yoga sessions, try just a few simple techniques. Not up for either of those? Try taking a simple walk. Go play some frisbee golf at a local course. This is a relaxing sport that is simply walking and stretching, working your muscles gently while giving your mind something else to focus on. If you don't have the time or the energy for either of those, then just sit for a few minutes and focus on your breathing. This is a state of mindfulness that puts you in the now and takes you out of the cycle of thought that can lead to a deterioration of your emotions.

Join a Support Group. Whether it's online or in-person, there are plenty of support groups available for people who are experiencing the exact same things you are. Reach out and connect. Know that you are not alone, and allow others who are going through the same thing help you. In return, it can be very beneficial and rewarding to listen to what others are experiencing and help them through it as well.

Attend Therapy. The best way to deal with BPD is to get the tools and experience under your belt for approaching your life from a much healthier mental and emotional standpoint. Therapy is by far the best tool available for those who have BPD. Childhood trauma is the most common reason for BPD to manifest. It makes sense to want to avoid going down that road and reliving those experiences. But the best road to any form of health is straight through it.

There are a few different therapy options available, most falling under the auspices of Cognitive Behavioral Training. One that has broken free of CBT and now falls under its own form of training that was originally created for the treatment of BPD, is Dialectical Behavioral Therapy. Most CBT training is done weekly or bi-weekly over a period of 1-2 years. DBT is a 9 month to 1-year program that meets once to twice weekly and is highly effective for giving an individual with BPD the tools they need for lifelong coping and management of their life.

If You Care About Someone with BPD...

Pay Attention to Warning Signs

Watch for signs of self-harming and emotional/angry behaviors. These are signs that your loved one is slipping into a very negative place. When they are not in the middle of these episodes, discuss their willingness to have these signs pointed out to them so that they may realize what is going on instead of living in a harmful or negative space. Every person is different, but in general, some of the warning signs to be aware of could be:

- They become too clingy and needy when you need space and try to set healthy boundaries.
- They become angry and lash out, making everything about you "bad" or "horrible."
- They criticize themselves and express feelings of worthlessness.

- They flip instantly through emotions, i.e. from calm/normal to screaming/ranting to sad/depressed.
- They start talking of life not worth living, or they have nothing left to live for.

Don't React, Stay Calm

Something major that can help someone with BPD is having someone listen to them and help them feel as though they are being understood. It helps to validate who they are, which they may be incapable of doing for themselves, especially when they are in crisis.

Be Kind and Honest

Ridiculing or calling someone with BPD out in a negative way for their behaviors will only heighten their emotional state, add stress to their state of crisis, and validate their feelings of unworthiness. Check-in with them to see how they are feeling and make sure that they know you care about them. Offer to help them through whatever they are experiencing or going through, but be specific with your offers to make the most of your help for their benefit.

Be Encouraging with Treatment Suggestions

BPD is a very complicated illness and can be frustrating for those who have it, as well as those who have to live with someone who has it. Suggest and encourage your loved one with BPD to begin and/or continue treatment, which is the only real way that they are going to find methods to recognize and moderate their negative behavioral patterns.

Work Toward Understanding Their Treatment

Take the time to understand what the treatment that is supposed to be helping your loved one is all about. Some of the treatment options are skill-based, like Dialectical Behavioral Therapy (DBT). Learn the language they are speaking, and the skills they are trying to implement into their lives, and yours, to make it a better living experience.

Chapter 3: Developing and Using Emotional Awareness

Those who live with Borderline Personality Disorder are governed by their moods and emotions for a large portion of their lives. Most of us are, but those who suffer from BPD deal with larger fluctuations, and a higher, disproportionate intensity of emotions than the rest of us do.

Just as we use what we know, have learned, and other aspects of our intelligence to assess what is going on with any given thing or situation, we also have an emotional awareness, which can be ascribed to as emotional intelligence. When we learn how to adequately access and use this intelligence, we can come to a place of understanding and action. No longer do our emotions have to control us; we can work to control our emotions and our responses to them.

We can start being "actionary" instead of reactionary. We learn to balance facts against emotional prejudices and programming. We learn to be empathetic to others' emotions and understand how our emotions are affecting them in a very real emotional way too. Tools and new programming are put into place so it can help us have healthier communication that strengthens our interpersonal relationships.

Increasing our emotional intelligence allows us to accept that negative feelings are valid and that instead of reacting to them and pushing them away, we need to take the time to examine them for what they are and what is or is not causing them. It allows us to have less emotional stress in our lives, and more positive emotions are felt more easily… laughter, playfulness, joy… it allows us to more fully enjoy life as a whole.

Emotional intelligence is defined by 4 attributes of awareness and management.

- Self-Management
- Self-Awareness
- Social Awareness
- Relationship Management

So, what can a deeper understanding of emotional intelligence do for us? Why should we become emotionally intelligent?

Improved Mental Health

Being unable to understand our emotions can make us stressed, and increases our vulnerability to depression, anxiety, and a wealth of other emotions. By learning how to understand our emotions, we can lower those levels of stress and develop stronger, healthier relationships with others… and with ourselves. Understanding our emotions is the first step in being able to accept and manage them, which increases the mental health benefits we can achieve.

When we are able to achieve lower stress levels, say, through meditation, it brings us to a more balanced and calm state where natural healing elements in our bodies take over. Exercising in small ways such as walking, swimming, or Yoga or Tai Chi as previously mentioned, produce what has been called stress-busting enzymes which lower levels of anxiety and depression, and can actually boost self-confidence levels.

Improved Physical Health

There are so many aspects of physical health that are affected by stress in our lives. What has a greater effect on our stress levels than emotions? Emotions play a major part in the levels of stress we have! How does that stress, in turn, affect our physical selves? It can raise blood pressure, which can increase the chances of strokes and heart attacks, contributing to heart disease. It can suppress immune systems which in turn leaves us more vulnerable to illness and infection. It can also age us, and make us more tired and run down. By getting a handle on the emotions and how they are allowed to interact in our lives, it can have an incredible impact, in a positive direction, on our physical state of health and well-being.

Improved Social Awareness

Being more connected to our emotions also helps us to better connect to others around us. We start to become more aware of things from a non-emotional standpoint and can better judge or become less judgmental of other people and their interactions with us, especially in a social environment. It helps us better empathize with others and identify who is being sincere, and who is not. We can start to recognize who is helping us and who might actually be causing more harm than good, and maybe why they are doing these things that affect us one way or another. This may help us to better understand how the way things that we do or don't do affect others. It also helps us to actually feel more connected, loved, and balanced through social interaction.

Improved Relationships

This is not only about romantic relationships, but also about family relationships, friendships, and other social relationships, including those we develop at work. When we finally begin to get a handle on our own emotions, we also start to recognize the validity of the emotions of the other people in our lives. Our communication skills improve, and we are better able to express ourselves in a way that is less damaging to ourselves and others. It can certainly be less damaging to the relationships in which we are involved.

With the benefits of emotional awareness in mind, let's step back and take a deeper look at those four stages of awareness and management again.

1. Self-Management

One of the hardest things for us to do at times is to manage our emotions. This can be especially true in times of stress. It is hard to control our emotions, or even think clearly when things get under our skin and bring our emotions flaring to life. By staying in the present, in the now, and focusing on what is not only causing our emotions, but our reactions to them, or to whatever it is that is stressing us out, we can start to be more focused on ourselves and learn to control our reactions to external stimuli as well as internal dialog. We are the ones to take control of our lives, build better relationships, and build ourselves into healthier individuals.

2. Self-Awareness

Attachment is a key influence in our own self-awareness. All too often, especially when we have had negative experiences as early as childhood when it comes to our emotions, we detach ourselves from emotionally feeling the unpleasantness of those memories and experiences.

The problem comes when we can no longer identify why we feel or react in a certain way to various situations because we have detached emotionally. It increases our stress levels, and our emotions start to take control, instead of us managing our emotions for healthier responses and reactions to situations. It is a difficult task to reconnect to our emotions, but by doing so, we are able to be present instead of reactionary to situations. Instead of trying to "read" what others are feeling and use that as a baseline for what emotions are supposed to look like, we can rely on our own feelings and be aware of them.

We learn to calm ourselves and evaluate what is happening and how we are feeling from a place of non-judgment. It is in this place of focused mindfulness, that we can start to make ourselves whole again, and become more connected, not only with ourselves and our emotions but with those around us.

3. Social Awareness

Being socially aware helps you to connect with the world around you, especially those you care about. Social awareness is being able to identify those little social cues that give you an empathetic insight into how someone else is feeling or reacting, even to how they are feeling and reacting to you. It helps to be mindful, at the moment, when it comes to social awareness.

This means being able to step outside your own head and the thoughts that are jumbled and whirling around, trying to think of how you feel in the moment, or reacting to what is going on. Instead, you become focused on the other person, and actually listen to what they are saying, and watching for their cues that connect with their words, or maybe recognize that their cues are in direct opposition with what their words are saying.

Are their words in harmony with their actions? What doesn't seem right, or feel off to you? The ability to key into how others around you deal with their emotional states can offer you great insight into your own.

4. Relationship Management

We have many different kinds and levels of relationships in our lives. The ability to be able to connect on a deeper level is part of the human experience. It is how we connect that can make a difference. We can learn to manage our emotions and relieve stress in our relationships, by relieving the stress and pressure we focus on.

Conflict is natural. It happens in every relationship. Without it, the relationship does not grow. It is when we can identify that conflict doesn't have to be negative, but can be a tool for compromise, understanding, and growth, that we begin to feel safer, opening up our more joyful and creative sides for moving forward in a healthy manner.

Other important factors to consider with relationship management are such things as mature communication. When we are not managing our emotions in a healthy way, they can cause us to react in less than healthy ways to conflicts that arise in a relationship, causing us to lash out instead of effectively communicate our feelings.

Empathetic understanding can be a key factor in this, learning how to listen to what the other person is saying and where they are coming from, instead of only viewing it from our own standpoint, or how we feel about the situation is a key factor in effective relationship management.

Relationship management has a better chance of success when both parties are on the same page. One way of doing this is to sit down and set goals for your relationship. You can start with little steps… Counting to ten when angry and evaluating what you say instead of just letting every little thing come out unfiltered, is an admirable, and a very healthy step toward a goal of effective emotional communication. Decide what you want your relationship to look and feel like, and set your goals. Decide on ways to be able to reach that goal. Be healthy and effective in the management of your relationship.

Emotionally Intelligent People Are…

Aware

This is not only true of their own feelings, but of the feelings of others. It is the recognizing of how emotions have an impact on our reactions. It is asking ourselves the tough questions… why am I feeling this way? What are my strong points and weak points when it comes to emotions? Is there a better way that I can react in a situation? How do my moods and emotions cause me to react?

Awareness helps us to see ourselves, and help us to understand how others may see us. The latter is a little more difficult, but we can learn to ask questions in a safe environment and learn from the answers we receive. Whether that dialogue is internal- or external-based, we learn to ask these questions without judgment and/or without condemning the answer. We evaluate the answer for what it is and see how it sits with us, and make our decisions based on that non-judgmental evaluation for our future emotional health.

Empathetic

Empathy allows us to put ourselves in someone else's shoes and take a spin around their emotions for a while. It is not always the actual feeling of what they feel, but it can be how we would feel in the same position. That isn't always the same. It doesn't mean that we necessarily agree with how they are feeling, but it is an attempt at understanding what they are feeling and why they may be feeling it.

Curious

Much like being aware, curiosity takes awareness to the next level. We are already asking ourselves the hard questions. Continuing to be curious and looking for answers heightens our awareness as we constantly strive for improvement. It is the being in the now and determining the answers that help us to become more confident in who we are and to be proud of what we can do to make ourselves even more amazing.

Poised

Whether it is to stop and take a pause before we jump in with both feet with emotional reaction, or just to stop and take a breath before we say something that can't be taken back, control in how we react in a situation is very important… and necessary, especially for someone struggling with Borderline Personality Disorder. Poise is also about what we do and don't allow to take root inside of our heads, it is a metered response to manage our emotions and maintain control of our own actions and reactions. When we are affected by something, our emotional reactions come instantly. It is an immediate, instinctive response to what is happening, and usually the first instinctive response we have, for better or worse.

By taking a breath, we can see how we are reacting, and maybe even allow that what we are reacting to is not worth allowing to grow in our hearts and minds. Just because we are hit with it, does not mean we have to let it stay. We choose what we want and don't want to spend our emotional energy on.

Equipped with Foresight

Similar to having poise, having foresight in situations where strong emotional responses can come into play in a situation, using foresight takes the instant emotional reaction and slows it down. It is about taking a step back before responding and trying to view the situation from a non-emotional, non-judgmental standpoint.

Through foresight, we try to look at what is happening as though from an outside, third-party viewpoint. We take a run through possible scenarios in our mind and evaluate what emotional response may be found with each outcome, or what response, emotional or otherwise, might get us the eventual outcome that we desire. Foresight allows us to choose the best-desired action for us to achieve what we want.

Adaptable

When we start to become more emotionally healthy, we not only recognize what we do and don't want to have in our lives, but we open ourselves to change in order to continue growing more and more healthy. We start evaluating needs vs. wants, and recognize that it is more important to prioritize those needs over our wants. We find the ability to recognize when something is working for us, or when we need to reevaluate and change those things that are not working.

Open to Criticism

This doesn't mean that we allow others to criticize us in an unhealthy way. It means that we listen when we are offered constructive criticism, and then make decisions on how we choose or choose not to apply it to our lives. It also doesn't mean that we have to make changes even when we are offered constructive criticism. It means that we don't react from a place of negativity when such criticism is offered. We are the captains of our own lives, and no one can make us live them in a way that we don't want to. However, constructive criticism is not meant as a means of attacking who we are or what we are doing. It is an offer and a potential opportunity of growing into a better version of ourselves. Something the emotionally intelligent is always open to.

Positive with Others

As much as our universe revolves around us, it does have other people in our orbits, and it helps to be positive in our interactions with them. For people who suffer from BPD, this can be especially difficult, because of all of the insecurities and fears circulating that lead toward unintentional destructive behaviors when others are around us. Just as we don't appreciate negative feedback and criticism, others don't either. It is not helpful for us and is not helpful for them. We need to remember to give encouragement, praise, and positive (or constructive) feedback and criticisms to those in our lives. We give what we want to receive.

Forgiving and Apologetic

These are two sides of a similar coin. Again, we are not the only people in the orbit of our universe. When we do something that negatively impacts another, we need to make apologies for our actions. Apologizing doesn't mean that we are 'wrong' or 'weak', it means that we are sorry for having made someone else feel the way that we did. We are not in control of how they feel, any more than they are in control of how we feel. It is important to remember that we are not the only ones with emotional value and validity in a relationship. Being able to apologize for your actions comes from a place of emotional maturity and strength.

Forgiving someone else is just as important as apologizing. And forgiveness is not just about making the other person feel better after doing what they did to harm us or impact us in a negative way. Forgiveness is just as important to us. When we have the capacity to forgive, it comes with it the capacity to let go of something that happened, and not allow it to have a continuing negative impact on our lives in the present or future. There is a good quote by Buddha that goes; *"Holding onto anger is like drinking poison and expecting the other person to die."*

Protective of Themselves

Emotional sabotage is a very real thing when it comes to those who struggle with Borderline Personality Disorder. By learning how to not react in an emotionally negative way, we slow the progressive tendencies toward emotional sabotage. The tendency of unhealthy emotional awareness is to manipulate others through emotions. At the same time, when in an unhealthy emotional state, we are also more easily manipulated by others through our emotions. By becoming more aware of our emotions and our reactions, we resist trying to manipulate others, while protecting ourselves from the same kind of manipulation in return.

An emotional consultant by the name of Jessica Moore once said:

> *"Emotional healing requires more than simply changing how you feel. Your emotions are merely symptoms of the problem—not the problem itself. Even when they hurt."*

When it comes to those who struggle with Borderline Personality Disorder, it is important to recognize that there is emotional healing that needs to take place as they work on developing their own emotional awareness. BPD is not something that just "happens", or comes into play via genetics. It is often an indicator of some deeply felt emotional trauma experienced when they were young.

It is natural for them to protect themselves from having to examine the what and how of what is happening with them and their emotions. What exactly is happening? How did this get to this point? The why is not asked here, only the what and how. There is no "why" that can adequately describe the trauma that has been experienced. The what and the how need to be addressed, but time can be taken to examine it slowly, little by little, as they are ready to touch upon each point for healing themselves and getting their lives back on a healthy track.

This is not an easy step, but it is a necessary one for long-term health on all levels, mental, emotional, and even in relationships with others. Until they can start becoming more aware of what their emotions are, and reconnect to these past events to discover how they were truly affected, recognize that this was through no fault of their own, and then reintegrate their emotional connection to the event in a healthier way, it will be difficult to step past the pain and reactions they have lived with their entire lives. Healing will be a continual struggle but it can be achieved, and awareness is the first step toward that healing.

Chapter 4: Treatments

There are quite a few options that are worth taking a look at for the treatment of BPD, even though they will not be the full topic of discussion. Later on, we will be taking a more in-depth look into Dialectical Behavioral Therapy since it is a very effective tool for working with someone who struggles with Borderline Personality Disorder.

Because the nature of BPD is so changeable, depending on the individual, there is no "one-size-fits-all" when it comes to helping those who struggle with this disorder. While DBT has proven to be one of the most successful when it comes to treating BPD, there are those for whom it may not work, or may only partially work. Since it is the major topic of discussion we want to offer, we can only hope that it works for those who have come seeking help within these pages. *If it does not...* we also want to be able to offer some other possible suggestions, to which you might turn to.

Medication

As discussed previously, there are no real medications approved by the FDA, that have been designated as helpful and/or successful to aid those struggling with BPD. However, also discussed before, BPD is a "surplus" disorder, with many different symptoms and signs that vary from individual to individual. Some of the individual symptoms might be of help or alleviated with certain medications, dependent upon the needs of the individual. It should also be noted that the treatment of BPD with medication should also be accompanied by some sort of therapy, as there is usually a deeper root cause of the onset of BPD.

Anti-Depressants

Depression can play a major part in those with BPD. While anti-depressants may not help with other emotions, such as anger, they can be successful in helping to treat symptoms of depression, sadness, general anxiety, posttraumatic stress disorder… all things which are possible for those with BPD to be experiencing in addition to everything else they are facing.

Anti-depressants can help individuals better balance their emotions, apply less focus to negative emotions, and apply more focus to positive emotions.

Anti-Psychotics

Before BPD was better understood, antipsychotics were among the first line of treatment for those diagnosed with this disorder. They are still offered today, in conjunction with therapy, for such aspects of mood affectation as paranoia, impulsive disorder aspects, and anger.

Anxiolytics

Some of the mood-related irrational behaviors brought out by BPD can be helped with these anti-anxiety directed medications, but BPD sufferers can also have addiction problems, and many of the anxiolytics can be highly addictive, so the value of what they provide for mood stabilization needs to be weighed against the addiction they can elicit.

Anti-Convulsant/Mood Stabilizers

Mood stabilizers, in addition to being beneficial by emotionally stabilizing an individual so that their emotional processing is less erratic, can be beneficial in helping to reduce impulsivity in those struggling with that aspect of BPD.

Cognitive Behavioral Therapy

As we discussed with the chapter on emotional awareness/intelligence, Cognitive Behavioral Therapy focuses on first becoming aware of emotional behaviors, reactions, and responses. Once awareness is achieved, this style of therapy then turns into helping the patient process and change their conscious ways of thinking, and the behaviors they exhibit that are visible to others.

Dialectical Behavioral Therapy

DBT works to help those with Borderline Personality Disorder to learn how to regulate emotions. It is done through group and individual therapy, mindful meditation, breathing techniques, muscle relaxing and identifying ways to change unwanted and/or negative behaviors. There is a focus on how beliefs and thoughts can directly lead to behaviors and actions, and how to manage conflicts and cope with the strong emotional impulses they experience. We'll get much further into this later on.

Schema-Focused Therapy

Schema-Focused therapy is a fancy way of saying that there are different classes of individuals and that each needs to be approached in a different way. The Schemas that are set to define Borderline Personality Disorder are those stemming from childhood trauma, and the resulting development of each: angry/impulsive child, the abandoned/abused child, the punitive parent, and the detached protector.

To achieve positive, lasting results, Schema-Focused therapy requires a minimum of two years of dedication. It includes assertiveness training, role-playing, and guided imagery. It works to help the individual get rid of the schemas that control their current life behaviors and reactions, and help them to find newer and healthier ways to cope with everyday life as an actual healthy adult.

Psychodynamic Therapy

Psychodynamic therapy works to discover those subconscious mental processes that develop during childhood and affect an individual's ability to function as a healthy adult later in life. It is usually a long-term, outpatient therapy that has had long-lasting effectiveness in those who struggle with BPD.

Transference-Focused Psychotherapy

Many people who struggle with BPD tend to be unable to differentiate their feelings and views of themselves, both positive and negative, from those around them. They transfer their own emotions and behaviors to those around them, unable to see how others may see or react differently in similar situations. Transference-based therapy helps the individual to identify when they are applying a transference of emotions to someone else, and help them to work through the understanding that others may process things in a different way.

Mentalization-Based Treatment

Mentalization-based treatment helps those who struggle with BPD to actually visualize their thoughts and emotions and to identify the thoughts and emotions of others and then visualize what those may look like as well. It helps individuals to better recognize what they are experiencing, and empathize with what those around them may be feeling and experiencing as well.

Systems Training for Emotional Predictability and Problem-Solving

Also referred to by its acronym, STEPPS, this program provides training for the individual in cognitively recognizing behaviors and emotions, and gives them the proper tools to manage and work with those emotions with and around others. In addition, it integrates training involving family and loved ones to provide them ways to work in a positive, productive manner with the person in their lives who struggles with BPD and teaches them the same techniques the individual is learning in therapy, so they can help to reinforce those positive methods and behaviors.

Hospitalization

Because Borderline Personality Disorder is not uncommon, and can deeply affect those who struggle with the intensity and depth of emotions that they experience, hospitalization to help stabilize them might be a genuine necessity. About 20% of those hospitalized for mental illnesses are those who struggle with BPD. Added to that, the high rate of those with BPD who self-harm or contemplate or attempt suicide can make it imperative to get someone struggling with BPD some intensive, in-patient care.

Self-Help

Self-help is an important aspect to becoming a healthier adult when struggling with BPD, but should not be done as the sole source of treatment. In almost all cases, those with BPD are much better served with help from a competent professional in getting the help they need to identify and redirect their emotions in a positive way.

That having been said, there are some things that can offer benefit in addition to therapy, that someone who struggles with BPD can take on their own. Self-help education is a huge benefit. Trigger the curiosity and keep it alive, always moving into a mindful position of self-awareness of emotions and state of mind. Studying cognitive coping skills for what they are going through can also be helpful.

From a natural standpoint, Mindful meditation, such as that you might find in the study of *True Buddhism*, with guided meditation and mindful awareness techniques, can be a very helpful addition to your toolbox. Essential oils such as lavender or chamomile added to your bath, sprayed on your pillow at night, or dabbed to your wrists or temples are said to have a calming effect on depression and stress. Even a simple change like creating routines for bedtime can have a relaxing and de-stressing effect on the emotions.

Borderline Personality Disorder has a lifetime effect, that may or may not lessen over time, but it doesn't have to be a negative one. Learning to balance your emotions, awareness, and relationships is a big step toward a lifetime commitment to taking charge of your life and allowing yourself to grow in a healthy, beneficial manner.

Chapter 5: Relationships and BPD

About 4 million people in the United States alone struggle with Borderline Personality Disorder. It can be an emotional roller coaster for those who have to live with it, whether the individuals themselves or anyone close to them… friends, family, and especially with romantic relationships. Despite the fact that those who struggle with BPD have such intense emotional dysfunctionality, most of those who struggle with BPD are very sweet, helpful, caring people, and can even exhibit personalities that have a strong magnetism that draws others to them.

They also struggle with very low images of self-esteem, and their feelings of emptiness leave them feeling as though there may not be enough love in the world to make them feel what a true relationship is all about. Because they don't feel their own self-worth, they seek to validate their worth by filling their lives with other people, trying to make the others value them in order to *feel* valued themselves.

Relationships can be a struggle, even when both adults are emotionally healthy or stable. There is no relationship that doesn't experience some kind of conflict, whether internal or external. No two people are exactly the same, and those differences will arise at some point and create a conflict. It is how the conflict is handled that makes the difference between a healthy and unhealthy relationship, and when involved with someone struggling with BPD, conflict often takes on a very unhealthy turn. That can be changed! But first, let's see what a relationship with someone who has BPD looks like.

People who have Borderline Personality Disorder crave intimacy, connection, romance, and close personal bonds with family and friends. They look for love and value outside of themselves, because they are disconnected from their own emotions and feelings of self-worth inside of themselves. They struggle and try to understand what this emotion is, and desperately want to achieve it, but often approach it in unhealthy ways, losing themselves in the process. And because they don't understand what they are looking for, what it is they *think* they should be feeling, they are continually left unsatisfied, alone with their feelings of emptiness, even when involved in intimate relationships.

Those who struggle with BPD have very intense fears of being abandoned. They also are greatly conflicted with fears of rejection. What might be a seemingly small incident for a loved one… brushing away a touch because they are in the middle of writing a term paper… might be perceived as intense as a *slap*… "don't touch me!" to someone who has BPD. They fear to reach out again because they fear the rejection they perceive as a possibility if they do. No one likes to be rejected but the feeling of rejection is super painful for the BPD sufferer. Their partner now doesn't understand why their loved one no longer reaches out and touches them, why there might be some hostility thrown into the mix. They don't comprehend how their subconscious action caused a shift in how their BPD loved one now perceives some of the nuances of their relationship. An ugly cycle starts, with both parties standing in the dark as to the true root of the problem.

Where most people see the colors of the rainbow and all shades in between in dealing with emotions and reactions and their personal interactions, a person with BPD sees black and white. It either is, or it isn't. They only see events and actions through their own perceptions of emotions and don't comprehend that others don't necessarily feel the same way. It is a very myopic view, but valid through their understanding of emotions, rejection, and feelings of abandonment.

There is no definitive answer as to what causes Borderline Personality Disorder, but it is believed to stem from deep-rooted trauma that they experience as children. There are people who have not experienced childhood trauma who also have BPD, but it is far less common. There is certainly a higher correlation between those with BPD and reports of childhood trauma, abuse, or neglect, especially when it involves their primary caregivers. Up to 76% of people who are diagnosed with BPD report some form of sexual abuse as children, while up to 73% have indicated some sort of physical abuse.

Child abuse can be defined in a wide range of behaviors-- mental, emotional, and physical, as applied to do harm to a minor. This can range from physical abuse, which can involve hitting, bruising, and broken bones, although it does not have to be that severe to still qualify as physical abuse. It can be sexual in nature, whether being involved in a sexual experience with someone older or even being exploited sexually by someone who is supposed to care and watch over you. It also can be defined as being mental or emotional in nature, suffering verbal attacks, yelling, screaming, being subjected to degradation or being degraded in some way.

It is certainly not easy to identify child abuse when it happens in fewer extremes, but the action and result are still felt in extremes by the child being subjected to the abuse. Sadly, there are other forms of abuse that are not so easily identified or caught by those who might otherwise help the child to get away from their abusers. Some of the more passive sides of abuse can include the denial of basic necessities, such as food, water, bedding, clothing… or denial of emotional needs and care… ignoring the child, not offering love and attention, emotional invalidation… these are all forms of abuse, none any less damaging than the other when it comes to the end result of long-term harm and damage to the child and how it shapes their emotional world into adulthood.

What does this mean for their future relationships with others? How are their perceptions and behaviors molded based on their earlier experiences?

Those with BPD suffer deep feelings of emptiness, unable to properly process emotions. Their deep-rooted feelings and fears of rejection and abandonment, and see it as a reality, even if they are really not being rejected or abandoned. They don't understand secure, healthy relationships, because they didn't have them in their formative years. The intensity of their fear causes them to act out in ways that actually push frustrated partners away, instead of drawing them closer, which is what they truly desire.

At the beginning of a relationship, those with Borderline Personality Disorder are very intense and passionate, making them very appealing to a prospective mate. They fall very hard, very quickly. They tend to jump into relationships without waiting to find out who the person really is and whether or not they are actually compatible. They idealize their partners and put them on pedestals, personifying them as the perfect mate.

The problem with all of this is that none of us are perfect. Those who struggle with BPD can go from white to black in an instant, without stopping to consider their partners, because, at that point, they don't feel their partners are considering them. A few minutes late on a call or arriving, not immediately responding to a text, not answering the phone right away… these are all things that can jumpstart the emotions of someone with BPD into overdrive, and send them spinning into a world entirely of their own making. They immediately feel the rejection and feelings of abandonment coming to the surface and act out accordingly.

At this point, it doesn't matter to them that their partner is running late because of traffic or an accident. It doesn't matter that their partner didn't call them right after they left work, because their boss held them up for a bit, and they hadn't actually left work yet. Driving or being in a place where phones are not allowed is no excuse at that moment for not responding to their texts or phone calls. This is the black and white world of someone who struggles with BPD.

This is not to say that they can't work through these issues and have a far healthier relationship. It is what the unhealthy side of BPD looks like. Someone who struggles with BPD has to learn how to integrate their emotions. They understand anger and frustration, but they try to avoid a deeper look at these feelings because they have detached from those kinds of negativity. The emotions bubble to the surface without them even realizing that this kind of negativity has taken hold and with their detachment from the emotions, they don't know how to integrate their loving feelings with their negative ones. Without that integration, it is an "on-off" switch that flips from one extreme to the other, instead of finding the balance and understanding of combining the two.

For partners in a relationship with BPD, it becomes highly important, if they want the relationship to survive, for them to learn and understand more about the disorder that has such a profound effect on their loved one. Many partners won't even know that their partner has BPD which can cause a range of different emotions in moments of conflict such as confusion, frustration, and exhaustion. Without being aware of the disorder their romantic partner has, there remains an expectation for their partner to behave in a normal manner.

With awareness and knowledge of the disorder, they can then begin to understand that it really isn't about the many of the things they really may or may not be doing. In reality, it is about the intense struggle with emotions that their loved one is experiencing, and that their loved one needs help to understand themselves, their emotions, and the disconnection that happens when they try to interact on any kind of personal level with other people.

When in a relationship with someone who has BPD, it is very important to remember that the way the partner views the relationship, and the way the person with BPD views it, can be remarkedly different. It is this perception that affects how they interact in their relationships with others.

Even their thought patterns reflect how they feel emotionally, not necessarily what is true and evident. The thing is, that to them, it *is* true and evident:

- *"No matter what I do, even in desperation, I lose everyone that I care about. People leave me because they don't care about me in the same way that I care about them."*

- *"I try and do whatever I can to make the way I feel go away. It is frustrating when I don't get what I need from someone else, and they don't understand me."*

- *"Unless I am loved every moment by everyone in my life who is important to me, it becomes obvious how worthless I am."*

- *"People wouldn't treat me badly unless I am bad, so if they are treating me badly, then I am bad."*

- *"I am nothing without someone else, so when I am alone, I do not exist. I am nothing."*

- *"Everyone is out to hurt me and I don't understand why. What did I do wrong?"*

- *"I feel lost and empty without someone else's love to fill me up."*

- *"I don't care if they have to work late, if I was truly important, they would be here with me."*

Not every individual with BPD has exactly the same symptoms or responds in exactly the same way. It is fair to say that these are common, albeit generalized, statements often made, felt, or expressed by those who struggle with BPD.

In a relationship with someone who has Borderline Personality Disorder, the partner may feel exactly the opposite of what the person with BPD thinks they do. Rather than argue, it becomes more important to understand that for someone with BPD, these emotions are very real, and these opinions are very valid. It is only by recognizing and acknowledging that these emotions and feelings do exist, that the two people in the relationship can work to find a way to combat and integrate these feelings, to become more aware, and learn healthier ways to recognize and manage the emotions to build a healthier relationship.

People with BPD are trying very hard to get their needs met. They tend to place unreal expectations on the others in their lives, but they don't see those expectations as being anything other than ordinary. It is important to note that most people who have BPD never had their needs met, even as children, so they do not recognize what it truly looks like, nor how to differentiate between need and want. To them, it is all the same.

Because of this, those with BPD will sometimes try to elicit a reaction, just to see what the reaction is supposed to look like, based on their perceptions. To their loved one, it can appear as though the person in their life with BPD is trying to manipulate a situation, or are being selfish and trying to gain their loved one's attention. In a sense they are, but they are not trying to do it to harm their loved one, rather, they are trying to find ways to get their needs met, with an inability to express their needs in a healthy way.

One of the things that make it appear as though the person with BPD is being selfish or manipulative, is that they have a lack of sense of boundaries. This can take different forms, from borrowing clothes without asking first, to taking money or gum from a purse or wallet to discussing topics that are inappropriate to touch on, too personal, too intimate for a given situation.

Ironically, a person with BPD will often misinterpret the behaviors and actions of others as being malicious and out to harm them. This is part of the feelings of unworthiness with which they struggle. When they act out against these perceived feelings, they don't intend to be hurtful, it is a reaction that comes from a place of fear. It can even include threats to harm themselves or commit suicide.

Often a partner is not even aware of what is going on with someone in their life who struggles with BPD. Without that awareness, the person with BPD is often left alone, perpetuating their feelings of not being worthy of love. Even with the awareness, unless both parties are willing to learn about BPD, and work through the challenges together, it can be a difficult struggle to maintain any kind of healthy dynamic in the relationship.

Borderline Personality Disorder is a greatly misunderstood illness, can be hard to work through with someone you care about and is difficult to treat. But treatment is not impossible!

Chapter 6: Confronting the Damage of BPD

In the previous chapter, we discussed some of the behaviors that can come when involved with someone who has Borderline Personality Disorder. There are other behaviors that can arise, but it needed to be reaffirmed here that with knowledge, time, and patience, a relationship can be had with someone who has BPD. It should also be noted, that working with BPD on your own can be difficult at best, and the help of a professional therapist will offer the most benefit when trying to navigate the many emotional bombs that can explode at any time, both known and unknown. Use the tools and suggestions provided here to supplement, not replace, getting professional help to find the way to a healthier individual and a healthier relationship.

BPD being called a "surplus" disorder is not far off the mark. There are so many different forms that it can take, but each individual is different in how it affects them, how they process their emotions, and how they react in any given situation.

There are other damaging behaviors that can affect a relationship, and sabotage the person who has BPD. One of these is an inability to commit. This can be for several reasons and can take on several forms.

With commitment issues, someone who has BPD can continually have relationships in various stages of development on the side. Cheating is not an uncommon behavioral trait for someone with BPD, although it is not always present. For the person with BPD, the idea of having one or more others on the side of a primary relationship gives them the security of knowing that if their primary partner leaves them, they are still not alone. It helps them cope better with their potential issues of abandonment.

Sadly, this can also include a series of lies to protect themselves and their behavior, and most of all, their emotions. This can be quite devastating for the partner of the person with BPD. All relationships go through a "Honeymoon" phase. In a relationship where one of the parties is affected by BPD, this Honeymoon phase can be even more ideal, intense, and rewarding. When these other behavioral traits start to manifest (which doesn't happen in all cases, but are a very real possibility), the actions of the individual with BPD can be both harmful and damaging to their partner, who is left confused as to what just happened in a situation where they didn't even realize anything had gone wrong.

This can all be quite overwhelming, both for the partner with BPD, and their loved ones. It becomes much harder when BPD runs concurrently with other mental illnesses, which can often be the case. As we've discussed previously, there are many symptoms of BPD that have crossovers with other mental illnesses. However, because of the nature of BPD and these crossover symptoms, it often develops alongside other mental illnesses that can either change the face of how BPD is presented or, at the very least, exacerbate some of the aspects of BPD that might have been less intense, otherwise.

Possible Concurrent Mental Illnesses/Disorders

Attention Deficit Hyperactivity Disorder (ADHD)

The occurrence of ADHD in those who already struggle with Borderline Personality Disorder is roughly 25%. This is, on average, about 5 times higher of an occurrence rate than happens in the general population who are not already dealing with the symptoms and behaviors of BPD.

Some of the symptoms of ADHD include; the inability to focus on details and making careless mistakes because of lack of attention, difficulty maintaining attention, difficulty with follow-through and organization, is easily distracted... especially by external sources, can be fidgety and restless, exerts unnecessary physical actions... even when sitting still is necessary, excessive talking and always moving or seemingly on-the-go, difficulty with not interrupting others... unable to wait for their "turn", can be intrusive in other activities.

When treating someone with ADHD, doctors often turn first to medications. This can be beneficial to those who suffer from ADHD, however, the type of medications used can exacerbate certain emotional behaviors for those who suffer from BPD combined with ADHD, such as increasing emotions, added aggression and anger, increasing impulsive behaviors, and even increase paranoid behavior. When the ADHD manifests in a milder form, therapies such as Dialectical Behavioral Therapy can be beneficial to treat both. Otherwise, it may be necessary to start a therapy such as DBT, then introduce medication for ADHD in conjunction with a low dose form of anti-psychotic medication to help reduce any potential exacerbation of BPD symptoms.

Panic and/or Anxiety Disorders

The occurrence of Panic/Anxiety Disorders in those who already struggle with Borderline Personality Disorder is roughly 50%. This includes those who have major panic attack episodes, PTSD, OCD, etc. Although heightened anxiety levels alone, without a major anxiety disorder diagnosis, comes in at a much higher rate. About 90% of those with BPD experience high levels of anxiety at one time or another.

Some of the symptoms of Panic/Anxiety Disorders can include increased heart rate, palpitations (with or without chest pains), trembling, shaking, sweating, shortness of breath or feeling sensation of being smothered, dizziness, feeling unsteady, nausea or other abdominal discomfort, being detached from one's self or from reality, tingling, numbness, overwhelming feelings of temperature like heat or chills, fears such as dying, going crazy, losing control, or going out among people or feeling trapped.

Behavioral therapy techniques such as those used with BPD can be very helpful for treating both sides of the BPD-Anxiety equation when found concurrently in a single individual. Medications are also very useful when treating Anxiety disorders, but which medications used are important. Some of the more commonly used medications for anxiety can increase impulsivity and can add to addictive behavioral issues. These include Valium, Klonopin, and Xanax. As with ADHD, the use of a mild or low-dose antipsychotic may be necessary when using medications to treat the anxiety disorder portion of mental illness when someone also has BPD.

Substance Abuse Disorders

The occurrence of Substance Abuse in those who already struggle with Borderline Personality Disorder is over two-thirds (66%). This can include street or prescription drugs and alcohol. These substances are often used in an attempt to avoid or dull emotions. The severity and intensity of their emotions are extremely painful, and such substances offer only temporary relief, but in turn, exacerbate the very emotions they are trying to escape.

Treatment for substance abuse is very necessary for those who have BPD. Without getting a handle on their substance abuse, there is little to no chance of their being able to get a handle on their emotions, and their cycles will continue to degrade in a very harmful manner.

Depression Disorders

Depression Disorders are exhibited in the majority of people who have BPD. These can be as serious as Major Depressive Disorder, or Bi-polar Depression, which can also come in conjunction with someone with BPD, and must be handled on a much deeper level.

Depression in BPD looks a little different than many Depressive Orders do when someone doesn't have BPD. Symptoms of a Depressive Disorder when experienced by someone with BPD almost always coincide with feelings of stress, or an event that triggers their depressive Disorder, and will often dissipate when those feelings of stress or life influences are resolved. These can include feelings of loneliness, sadness, and depression connected directly to fears of abandonment and emptiness. Suicidal thoughts and thoughts of self-harming can also be present, along with sleep and appetite disturbances.

The upside is that, as stated, these depressive feelings will often go away when the root cause dissipates. They are also effectively managed with techniques and skills that can be used to identify and manage stress and emotions, such as Dialectical Behavioral Therapy. Other Depressive Disorders that can come in conjunction with BPD and can benefit greatly from DBT, are Post Traumatic Stress Disorder (PTSD), and behavioral eating disorders such as Bulimia and Anorexia.

Narcissistic Personality Disorder

Dealing with someone who has both Narcissistic Personality Disorder (NPD) and Borderline Personality Disorder is far different from dealing with any other mental illness combined with BPD. It is also one of the most difficult combinations with which to deal. The statistics can be a bit skewed, because of the nature of someone with NPD. If you look at the numbers of people who are diagnosed and seek treatment for both, the numbers seem relatively low, comparatively speaking with other mental illnesses… 16%. However, one of the traits of someone who has NPD is that they don't feel they are in need of help or treatment. When the numbers outside of those who actually seek treatment are tallied, the comorbidity rate jumps to almost 40%.

It is difficult to diagnose the combination of NPD with BPD. They are often diagnosed in patients as one or the other. They do share a lot of common, or at the very least, similar symptoms and behaviors. On the other hand, some of the symptoms and behaviors are seemingly opposite to each other. They are not, really. The symptoms and behaviors that may seem to be in opposition, are usually so on the surface. What takes place in the minds and emotions of those experience these mental illnesses, is in actuality, very similar. Sometimes the opposite is true. What may look similar on the surface can come from a very different perspective, depending on which side of the mental equation is stronger.

We have discussed the deep-rooted fear of abandonment and self-worth issues of those who have BPD. When NPD is added into the equation, instead of the behaviors coming from a place of fear and lack of self-worth, the behaviors now can come from a place of deep manipulation, always trying to achieve the results they need and feel they deserve. In the case of NPD, all is fair game to achieve their desired end result, and they do not feel they are doing any wrong.

And therein lies the true problem when NPD is combined with BPD. Those with BPD need to seek treatment, while those with NPD do not feel there is anything wrong with themselves to seek treatment for. Individuals who struggle with BPD have a lack of sense of identity, whereas NPD people have an over-inflated sense of identity and feel that their desires are the only ones that truly matter. Combining the desperation of someone with BPD with the ego-centric NPD can be very harmful. BPD sufferers hurt themselves, and in lashing out, hurt others. For this, they feel remorse. NPD sufferers live behind a false-mask as a way of coping with the suffering, hurt others more than themselves, and don't care what they do. This is an extremely destructive combination for those who are in a relationship with another who has this combined mental illness.

The truly negative side for those who have NPD combined with their BPD is that those with NPD not only don't recognize the need to seek help, there is currently no medication or therapy that has been found to be effective in helping those with NPD. It can even develop into the stronger side of the BPD-NPD combination, should the BPD start subsiding in later years, as can be the case. Then the NPD comes out in a stronger, even more, damaging form, leaving those around them struggling to understand the drastic changes in their loved one.

A relationship with someone who has BPD can be daunting, and fraught with anxiety and confusion for both parties. When one or more other mental illnesses are attached, it can become even more so. Awareness and understanding are vital for the possibility of a healthy relationship, but awareness and understanding can be extremely difficult to achieve for a BPD sufferer combined with NPD.

Chapter 7: DBT to the Rescue

We have now discussed a lot of what can occur in and out of relationships with someone who has DBT. We have also discussed some skill sets that can be useful, and some of the options for treatment. The one treatment that stands out above the rest is Dialectical Behavioral Therapy (DBT). So…

What is DBT?

Let's start by breaking it down. Dialectical refers to the combining of two seemingly opposite ideas. In the case of DBT, these opposites are **Acceptance and Change**. In DBT, patients are taught to accept things the way they are right now, at this moment, without judgment. Then they look to what change can be made to their behaviors, reactions, how they do things, to make things better in their lives. It is looking at the concept of accepting that at this moment, they are already doing the best that they can, and they can continue to do even better.

Behavioral refers to the actions, reactions, and traits that they exhibit. Behavior can be trained. It is all about Reinforcement and Reward. Whenever we do something, and a result happens from it, that behavior is reinforced. A dog sits for you and is given a treat. This is not about reward, but reinforcement. They come to realize that if they sit (the behavior), they will be given a treat (reinforcement of the behavior). If an individual throws a temper tantrum, and the other person gives in to their demands, the temper tantrum (the behavior) gives them the result that they want (the reinforcement). So, reinforcement can work both to the positive and the negative, dependent upon how and when it is applied.

A reward is a form of reinforcement, but the thought is applied to a benefit achieved when good behavior is exhibited. This is not necessarily the case. In the eyes of the person exhibiting negative behavior tactics to achieve want they want, getting what they want is also the reward. Any behavior can be reinforced or rewarded, which increases the possibility that the behavior will be repeated.

In DBT, negative behaviors are targeted for change and reinforcement/reward. These can be anything from suicidal thoughts and thoughts of self-harm to over-indulgent behaviors with food and/or substance abuse, to reckless and impulsive traits. When the patient starts to have a better understanding of the bigger, more imminently harmful behavioral traits and how to modify their behaviors, then they can work on the smaller ones, which can be also very harmful to the person and their loved ones. Each person is unique in what those traits are and how they manifest.

The T is, of course, for Therapy. This is a huge part of DBT, because therapy, in its many forms that it will take during the course of a DBT program, is essential to the reinforcement of positive behavioral changes and skill-building. It takes a lot of coordinated effort between an individual and their therapist in order to build the shiny new toolbox filled with the skills needed to effectively change their lives for the better.

Altogether, DBT helps to teach individuals with Borderline Personality Disorder (among others) how to regulate their emotions, find healthy coping mechanisms for dealing with stress, how to live in the "now" of the moment, and how to improve their relationships with the people around them.

Effectiveness of DBT

Dialectical Behavioral Therapy was first developed in the 80s, by Dr. Marsha Linehan. It was initially developed for use with those who struggled with Borderline Personality Disorder. Those who struggle with BPD were found not to benefit as greatly or respond as well to traditional cognitive behavioral therapy of that time. Not only have they found DBT to have a much higher success rate with BPD, but it has also become an effective treatment for many other mental disorders and illnesses as well. Now DBT is included in many successful forms of Cognitive Behavioral Therapy (CBT) lists.

While highly effective as a form of CBT as DBT is, it is a difficult process for many to follow through on all of the ways. It is a great deal of commitment to time and work on the part of those who want to improve their lives, and also with the partners who want to be there for them. The numbers of those who start versus those who follow through and finish the program are less than 50%. In some cases, those numbers can run even lower, depending on the commitment of those who enter the program.

With that in mind, as high as 77% of people who get through their first year of DBT can actually eliminate the behavioral criteria that define BPD. This means that they have effectively worked to make BPD a non-influencing factor in their lives! It greatly reduces suicidal and self-harm behaviors reduces the number of inpatient hospital stays and lowers the levels of stress in their lives with management techniques for their erratic emotions.

The Way DBT Works

Before a patient is even entered into a DBT program, there are some agreements that must be established and worked on. Without this present from the start, the process has little chance of succeeding. First, the patient must agree to work with the DBT program for a minimum specified amount of time, and within reason, not miss any sessions. This can be as long as needs to be set out, but usually, the minimum falls around 9-12 months.

If the person with BPD has suicidal and/or other self-harm tendencies, they must agree to dedicate themselves to reducing those behaviors. They must be consistent with their skills training to develop the tools that will be used during therapy, and after therapy ends. The final establishment is that if any "therapy interfering behaviors" manifest, the patient must be willing to accept that these are not allowable, and must work to eliminate them for their effective treatment.

After this base is established, there are a few precepts that the therapist works to establish with patients who have BPD and are attending therapy. The first is that the patient is in therapy because they want to change, and regardless of how they feel, they are doing their best at any given moment. The second is that behavior patterns as they are currently exhibited are understandable, because of what has happened in their past. Life may not feel as though it is worth living, but suicide is not an acceptable solution. Rather, the true answer is to make life better so that it becomes worth living.

It is important for the individual with BPD to understand that they need to work hard in order to make the improvements they are looking for in their lives. How their lives are in the now may not be their fault, but they need to accept the responsibility that the only way it will change is if they work to make that happen. Lastly, the therapist helps the patient to understand that if things are not improving, it is the therapy failing the patient. The patient does not fail in DBT.

There are three settings under which DBT takes place. There is the classroom, where DBT teaches the patient's skill sets and tools for them to use. Actual homework assignments are given, and patients role-play to learn new techniques and behaviors for dealing with other people.

Individualized therapy is the second part, where the therapist works with the individual nature and behaviors of the patient to target what can work specifically for them.

Phone coaching is a very important third part, where the therapist is available to the patient via phone 24-7. This is to help with specific situations as they arise and make demands on the patient's skills. The therapist can help walk the patient through what they need to do and help reinforce those skills until they become second nature.

It should be noted that therapists who work with BPD through DBT are highly dedicated individuals, and they have to be. It is a very deep connection formed, which can be draining if they allow it to be. This is not a negative reflection on their therapeutic relationship with the patient, DBT is just a very intense process for both patient and therapist. In order for therapists to maintain their high level of patient care, it is necessary for them to connect with a consultation team of other therapists, in order to maintain a fresh perspective and motivation for a very difficult treatment.

There are four main strategies used by therapists to treat their BPD patients through the use of DBT.

Mindfulness

This is the process and practice of staying in the present moment.

69

Focusing on the now, one thing at a time.

Distress Tolerance

This strategy teaches the patient to accept and tolerate the stress factors and events in their lives as they happen, and how to review them for their future betterment. Surviving and/or tolerating crises in their lives are approached by several techniques to the strategy… focusing on pros and cons, distracting themselves, ways to improve the moment, and how to self-soothe in order to reduce extreme emotional swings.

Interpersonal Effectiveness

This strategy teaches the individual how to work toward healthy balances in their relationships with others, including how to say "no", and how to express their needs in a healthy way to be met without the reinforcement of negative behavioral patterns.

Emotional Regulation

This strategy helps the patient to work toward positive emotional responses and behaviors, creating better life experiences by recognizing and then managing their negative emotional responses, such as anger or frustration. By doing so, the patient learns to reduce their emotional vulnerability when dealing with others and can experience much healthier responses and relationships.

DBT requires a strong commitment on the part of the therapist, and also on the part of the patient. This commitment will be consistently evaluated and re-established during the course of treatment. The end results, when the work is put in, can be an amazing path to a new way of living for an individual who struggles with BPD, and the loved ones who struggle alongside them.

Support as a Partner

If your relationship partner with BPD is attending Dialectical Behavioral Therapy, there are a few things that you can do to help. Most often, DBT is a setting where they can speak freely and then learn how some of their words, emotions, and actions can be examined from a different perspective so that they can effectively manage themselves with DBT training. There are some DBT groups that are specifically for families or couples learning together how to cope with how BPD affects their relationships, so that is an option if you choose.

In addition, even regular DBT for the individual involves homework assignments, and attendance, both of which are mandatory for the therapy to work. The therapist and the rest of their DBT group hold them accountable for both, and you can help your partner by holding them accountable for doing the work and making the most out of their efforts.

You can also discuss their training with them, to understand what is involved, and help them hold to the tools that they are developing, such as rephrasing when using the words "would, should, or could," which are considered judgments. DBT tries to avoid judgements and simply look at facts. Help your partner avoid these judgment pitfalls and learn how to look at things without the emotional judgment quality involved, for example.

Helpful Techniques

Some of these techniques may seem overly simplistic, and some may seem as though they are just plain common sense. When you look at how an individual with BPD sees the world, they can actually be valuable tools to help them understand the way they are processing or to steer them away from circular logic and try to break old habits and old cycles. Some of them come from DBT itself, and others from a technique called non-violent communication, where you try to achieve understanding without accusation, but more with gentle persuasion.

Every relationship takes work. To be in a relationship with someone who has BPD takes even more work, and it is work that needs to be done by both parties, even more so on the side of the person who struggles with BPD. Dialectical Behavioral Therapy can be very beneficial for those with BPD, although it does take time and work to implement the techniques. Here are a few things that can help, especially if you are partnered with someone who has BPD, that can get you started, while the DBT skill development sets in.

Spread Positivity
Feeling that we are loved and that we have value is important for any of us. It brings relaxation, happiness, and helps create a less stressful environment.

Early Exits
When it looks as though your loved one is gearing up for an argument, try a polite exit to get something to drink, a snack, or to go to the restroom. Don't return until you have given it a few minutes and calmed yourself. When you do go back, try shifting the topic to something less intense, and then slowly find your way back to the other conversation, if it is something that needs to be addressed, rather than just left be. And only if it looks as though it is a conversation that can be managed without escalation.

Perspectives in Listening
One of the things that can quickly escalate into an argument is if one or the other person does not feel as though they are being heard.

Try repeating what they have said back to them, like a parrot, and then reword as to your understanding and ask if that is what they meant. If not, try repeating again, and rephrasing, until the other partner feels as though you understand what they are saying.

If it is you who feels as though they are not being heard, try a revision of the same technique. Repeat what the other person is saying back to them, letting them know that you are hearing them. Then try, "…at the same time…" and repeat what you are trying to get across, or rephrase what you are trying to get across.

Also… set aside your cell phone, turn off the television. Let your partner feel as though you are actually listening. Be present. Nod, use well-timed words such as "yes," or "uh-huh". It is not about agreeing with what they are saying, but letting them feel as though they are being heard.

People with BPD cannot always articulate what it is they are trying to tell you. Their emotions can make a confusing jumble of their thoughts. Instead of just focusing on their words, focus on the emotions behind what they are trying to convey. It may tell you a different story, and better help you get to a place of understanding with your partner.

In addition to self-help, individual and group therapy involvement, couples' therapy is something that should be strongly considered when one of the parties to the relationship struggles with a mental disorder but can be very effective to help a relationship grow into something healthy and long-lasting. When both parties are heard and can get the tools and skills they need to help themselves and their partner at the same time, a relationship becomes much more stable, and better yet, you can see and feel the positive benefits take root.

Chapter 8: High-Speed DBT

Dialectical Behavioral Therapy is not mastered in a quick chapter. It takes time. Lots of time and effort.

Repetition is part of why it takes so long to input the skills that will cope with any symptoms.

It also takes time because the skills we will talk about here are not as simple as what is written. This is more attuned to the first aid of relationships and how to survive.

Any skill that is related to DBT has value. And the application of that skill is valid no matter how much time has been spent learning it. The only concern we state here is that DBT requires individual time to achieve personal stability so that we can work on others, or better yet, ourselves.

With this in mind, there are many skills that can be used right out of the box, so to speak. We are going to focus on those that will get the most help on the table without advanced training.

It is in the advanced training that DBT shines.

One reason why DBT requires time is that it truly requires an outside reference. What this means is that we need sponsorship at our beginning undertaking. No matter what side of the BPD relationship the individual is on, having an outside advisor/therapist makes us healthier. This is the time required to properly achieve the skills to save us. When and if things get too far out of control for those involved to be safe, it is time for a pro to mediate.

Diving into the deep end of months of training *is* possible. We are going to attempt it. Like DBT states over and over again, the forgiveness of self will make ourselves more okay, and with the ability to do better.

There is a way to speed up the process. We are going to accomplish this by cherry-picking what skills will best gain results for applicable symptoms of the individual struggling with BPD. This means that not all of the steps or techniques listed here may apply to everyone reading this. Find the symptoms that the BPD individual struggles with, and focus on those. Do not omit the others, they may have benefits of which may not seem applicable. Learn to use, or at least have ready, every tool available to create a healthier emotional environment. We are also going to look at what the other side of the relationship can do and cannot do.

So, what does high-speed DBT look like? First, we are going to skip past initial mindfulness. This will be covered in a later chapter. We are going straight to coping skills. Mindfulness will become an accent to the skills we will be applying.

There is another way to speed up the process and that is to go straight to the meat. Or veggies, based on your choices. The application of the skill will become more essential than the why of the skill. Of course, we will be discussing the why of what skill applies to what symptom, however, we will not be getting into the full training of what that skill is and why it applies to our dialectical behaviors.

In fact, we will be looking at skill applications more than how to balance both sides of us. This is okay for the moment, only because we will be covering this a little bit in the mindfulness section.

Skills applied will help with the health of a relationship more than the philosophy of why we are what we are. Hopefully, some of those answers were at least touched upon, providing deeper insight for those seeking help in the previous chapters.

So here we go, basic training on our dialectical behaviors and what we can do to survive them. Everyone has a duality of logic and emotion. DBT focuses on defining emotions and using logic to understand them and apply the skill. The logical side of the equation is not truly examined. What this means is that we will be looking at emotional regulation more than logical regulation, using forms of logic to regulate the emotions.

We are emotional beings. Those with Behavioral Disorders deal with out of control emotions more than out of control logic. Well, that is not entirely true. An individual with a bipolar existence can have major out of control logic.

DBT works with out-of-control logic with a simple solution. Let go. This letting go is a high-speed way of dealing with the logical brain and allows it to have a new task of examining emotions.

Logical regulation is still in the future.

The runaway emotions of those suffering from Borderline Personality Disorder is more prominent, and more immediately treatable. We are going to head to strength and speed versus the slow and logical game of chess.

With that in mind, we are going to start to focus on the emotional side of our lives. Wisdom comes when we examine both sides. This is optimal in a relationship that is emotionally unstable. Wisdom comes from a blend of logic and emotion. DBT leans heavily on the emotional side of mental health.

There is no mistake. Those who are mentally unstable to the point of harming themselves and/or others are dealing with out of control emotions. Those we will look at in this text and examine some skills that can help. Just remember that those who are BPD are dealing with out of control logic as well, and hopefully, psychology will match up to philosophy, mix in some programming logic, and get in some logic therapy.

For now, we focus on the emotional stability of those suffering, including ourselves. The skills put forth come from practicing. It is in our nature to surrender to failure. Failure keeps us from trying again. Fear of failure kills our minds.

It is this that is the hardest lesson of DBT. It is the main reason that there is an attrition rate in the DBT class of dropouts. Fear and failure. One emotion and one logic.

The advice needed here is that we do fail, especially when trying new things. Now that we are speeding up DBT to help in the now, failure can happen. Remember… It is not the individual who is failing, rather it is the therapy failing the individual. This can be especially hard to overcome when approaching it in the manner we are in the here and now, without the therapy to back it up. The therapy portion is essential!

How we deal with this failure is how we deal with life. It is totally understandable that we can curl up in a ball and quit. But what happens when we don't?

What happens when we perceive failure? Do we learn? Do we improve? Do we know and understand how to avoid the same failure in the future?

This is the strength of DBT. Failing and then to keep going. This is not something that can be pressed on another. The best soldiers are not pressed into service, they volunteer.

That is what we must do now. Before any application starts. We must volunteer. If you, the reader, are not in a place where you are committed to learning and understanding that we can fail here and need to get back up, this may not be the proper avenue of skill set learning for you.

It is in the bravery of volunteering ourselves to something that may help us in the field that makes us better. One must volunteer.

So, all of us are on the page. It is time to get help. We are in need of emotional healing. We volunteer for this assignment knowing we may fail.

We learn, no matter what happens, because we commit.

A commitment to mental health through knowledge and application and work.

Here we go.

Chapter 9: Matching Skills from DBT to Symptoms of BPD

Many of the symptoms of personality disorders are not diagnosable in the mental health we currently practice today. The field does, however, see symptoms as something they identify and address.

What is meant by this, is that every case of any disorder is unique. Also, we must take into account that you may have a symptom or a series of symptoms and yet still no real diagnosis. This is acceptable and understandable because, in fact, we are very complex beings.

We will break down some of the symptoms for BPD. What needs to be kept in mind is that symptoms are NOT a diagnosis.

There are DBT skills that can help with any symptom, whether it is connected to BPD or not. So, let us grab a symptom and give it a try.

Fear of Abandonment, or the Terror of Being Left Alone

There are many forms of abandonment. Everything that ranges from emotional abandonment, all the way down to a child being abandoned in a train station. Each and every condition that brings about the fear of abandonment also brings about anxiety. This anxiety can spread to current relationships. The individual who is experiencing this cannot get the voices to stop saying the same thing. You are going to be abandoned.

Fear of being abandoned has a long-term effect. It makes the individual very sensitive to criticism. Any little piece of criticism brings forth a wave of reminders that they were once abandoned and will be abandoned again. Criticism is not necessarily a positive concept, to begin with, and the individual who has symptoms of abandonment will magnify every little statement.

This fear will make it very hard for them to trust others. The constant uncertainty as to whether "this will be the time" alienates them. They find themselves very alone unless they are certain that a friend or lover likes them in a way in which they feel secure. It is in this need of all bases to be covered that, the individual with a fear of abandonment, drives others away.

In this extreme constant justification that everything must be in order before committing to any relationship, causes the individual to take measures to avoid rejection or separation. This rejection or constant prejudging of what it means to separate causes a pattern of unhealthy relations with others.

To combat this fear, the individual attaches to people too quickly and then moves on just as quickly. A series of relationships fall into the wake of the life of the abandoned. Mostly caused due to the inward cycle. This cycle is out of control for the individual when left unattended.

To compensate for this fear, the individual works very hard to please the other person. They do this for multiple reasons. One is that so they can be justified when they are abandoned. Another is that so they can show their partner what they want by doing for them. This only works when there is communication between the two involved and normally the person suffering from fear does not communicate what they are doing. They just do it.

When the fear of abandonment finally manifests into reality, the individual does very little but blame themselves. It is in this self-regression caused by the fear that no one can do anything except blame themselves for everything that has happened. It is a self-fulfilling prophecy that fear leads to doubt and doubt leads to failure. Ultimately, the failure is caused by fear.

And the cycle whirls away in madness.

A final indicator that someone has a fear of abandonment is that they will stay in a relationship that is not healthy or possibly even harmful. When one wakes up next to someone who abuses them, they have choices. Accept, fight or walk. The individual who lives in fear will resort to acceptance in most cases.

The DBT skill that applies to fear is twofold. One part of this is to look at what is happening in a non-judgmental way. This non-judgmental way of living is essential to DBT skills. It is something that can really only come from vigilance and a professional mediator helping. We fall into self-judgment all the time. Yet, this is not the skill we are going to apply to fear of abandonment.

First, we must break down the experience into facts. Then we examine each of those in a way that separates each fact from every other fact. Each with its own merit. Those that are thoughts and not actual facts need to be removed from the table. This is not an easy task, as our thoughts do not just stop on a dime. Remember that we are not talking about opinions, for opinions are almost always valid. We are talking about separating fact from thought.

When we ask the questions about what is *actually* happening to us, and not just our *thoughts* about what will happen to us, we begin to see that we have to pause for any thought we have. The facts of what is *actually* happening to us are the only thing we need to base abandonment on.

Are we truly being abandoned or are we just thinking that we are?

Once facts are on the table, so to speak, we can begin to take action. We are going to apply the opposite action. This is the second skill that can be applied from DBT.

Opposite action is forcing or doing the opposite emotion to what one is experiencing. In the case of fear of abandonment, we are not saying hope of abandonment. We do not want to be abandoned. We are saying the opposite of fear.

Hope.

Once an individual who has fear of abandonment has looked at the facts of what is actually happening, they need to consider that the emotion that they are experiencing may not be a true representation of the facts. In other words…

Individuals with fear of abandonment need to practice radical emotion reversal by replacing every fear moment with **hope of love and connection**. The mind will only get changed with repetition here. A one-time attempt will not undo a lifetime of fear. Training is required, and that is what we are doing. We are training ourselves not to live in fear.

Let's try an example to help make this a little clear, and give you a tool to put into your toolbox for self-help and healing.

You send a text to a loved one at work, talking about spending time with them when they are done. Or, it doesn't even have to be talking about spending time together, it can just be a simple, "Hi! How is your day going?"

There is no response.

When dealing with fear of abandonment issues, this can start our thoughts and emotions down a slippery slope into anger and depression.

"Why doesn't my partner respond?"

"Do they not care about me?"

And so on…

Instead of focusing on the negative aspects of what might be running through our minds at this point, we need to stop judging the situation, when we don't know what may actually be going on.

"My partner is at work. They may be busy. They may not have heard my text…"

None of this truly matters we are only trying to bring a little outside awareness into our negative thinking at this point. Then we focus on the positive, and the hope of love and connection. We remind ourselves what makes us worth being loved.

"I let them know that I am thinking about them."

"I am a caring, loving person."

"I am understanding and sympathetic to the needs of others."

"I am deserving of love and happiness."

Focusing on the good of who we are, not only in stressful situations, but overall, and as often as we can, reminds us of how we deserve love and being in a relationship, and relieves the pressure to try and be more than the amazing person we already are. It reduces that emotional pressure and allows us to relax into being ourselves.

Unclear or Shifting Self-Image

Who am I? is a question often asked by those who are afflicted with BPD.

When someone does not have a self-image, they have no real anchor for when life goes sideways. The image of self is not something that comes easily. In fact, there are those who believe that we are nothing and we are going to nothing, and this is just as valid as someone who has a strong self and belief.

When we do not have a strong sense of self-image, we are in a state of constant flux about what is going on around us, and we begin to lose a grip on reality. It is in this uncertainty that we react so violently to the most mundane. It is the inability to understand ourselves that is projected outward in a way that we just cannot understand anything anymore.

The symptom is not that the individual has a question about who they are, more that they cannot comprehend that their personality changes so drastically from event to event.

First of all, from a non-DBT place, an individual can be as much or as little as they want to be. There is no right or wrong way to be.

And in this judgment of right and wrong, we find our skills can be used.

The individual who has difficulty with self-image can find their self-image by removing judgment. In this case, the opinions of yourself and others may not be valid. When we think of the self as in "this part of ourselves is right", and "this part of ourselves is wrong", we are judging ourselves.

DBT shows us that we are who we are. Flat. Of course, outside influences make us who we are. It is up to us to remember that we are allowed to change. We are allowed to be different. When those outside of us say things about our personality that ring true, we need to take a moment and look at ourselves.

It is totally acceptable to change one's personality to fit a situation. Everyone does this to a certain degree. It is the extremeness of the BPD that makes self-doubt creep in, and then identity is lost.

Sense of self is regained by implementing the skill of acceptance. The fact is, all of us change somewhat to fit our situations. Those with a greater skill to do this are labeled as extreme, and sometimes even treated harshly because everyone wants the steady.

Self-worth comes in time. DBT tells us that any self that we are is ok. It tells us that our self will change, and is changing moment by moment. Let go of opinions inside and out. Let yourself be.

Remember that it will take a great amount of time to find self.

While individuals suffer from the symptom of not having a self, they are subject to judging themselves with the feeling that they do *not* have a self. This can be a slippery slope. For in finding self, one must understand and accept that they have no self at the moment.

It is recommended that one looks at themselves to see and recognize that they have a changing self. This is the start, and very well may be the ending. It is a blessing to be able to change oneself to fit situations. It is as primal as animals surviving.

Just do not judge yourself, for being yourself, while, or after, you are.

Impulsive/Self-Destructive/Risk-Taking Behaviors

Those suffering BPD can have destructive tendencies. Those tendencies are impulsive. It is in this impulsivity that we learn the difference between being destructive and being impulsively destructive.

What if feelings were something that we could not control? And in fact, controlling feelings and emotions could be harmful instead of helpful? This is a philosophy in DBT, and it applies to risk-taking.

Feelings are not something we can really control. We can only control the situation around them and the extremeness of them. We have emotions for a reason and are not necessarily supposed to just turn them off.

The human condition is a series of break downs and build-ups. We destroy all the time. It is in how we do the destruction that we begin to see symptoms of personality.

Individuals struggling with BPD continuously test the waters, so to speak. They have had more than one experience in that they have tried something on impulse and received a reinforced, or "true" result.

For example, one does something radically different and possibly harmful to someone they love to see if they will stick around.

87

Harm is nothing new to those who question self. There is a philosophy of mind that thinks, "If I can be harmed then so can others". The test of the symptom is the symptom itself.

It is in this explosive destruction that the individual who questions who they are can get answers. To make something happen and to get a result from this happening is a way of seeing how others react so that "normal" can be found.

Unfortunately, a person with personality disorders does not stop there.

Impulse is not a one-time game. Risk-taking is just another way of being impulsive. Risk-taking is mostly about control. We take the risk to calculate. We take the risk to feel when we do not. We take risks to get excited. There is a part of us that also takes risks to lose. The more we risk, the more we feel alive, and if things go sideways, the more we can lose.

Therefore, the more risk we take, the more we feel—sometimes doubled, or even tripled. This is the same way we can feel when we act impulsively.

Risk-taking and impulsiveness can be extremely addictive. Most individuals who harm themselves have addictive personalities. Risk-taking is merely another feed into that persona.

Best advice to those who take risks, and those who do it without a semblance of self or the harm it can do to them or others, is to try not to. Unfortunately, there is always a semblance of risk in life. If you have to take risks, be mindful of the risks you are taking. Does it have a potential benefit to the outcome? Be aware whether the risks you take are beneficial or harmful to yourself or others.

That is correct. Risk-taking may indeed need to be treated like any other addiction. This is something that DBT helps within a way that a twelve-step process cannot. DBT is a complex program that should be done under the supervision of someone who understands the entirety of the process.

We can give you techniques, and help you understand some of the skills involved, but a large part of the program involves interaction with a therapist who can walk you through the process of understanding what you are doing and how it affects you and others. They can really help you to identify harmful behaviors and work with you on techniques specific to you for dealing with each circumstance in your life as it arises. About six months into the program, one begins to see the positive and negative effects of risk-taking on their lives.

BPD individuals know the concept of extreme. Applying extremeness to something that should be limited is power, and we can lose ourselves in that power, or to that power.

This is where DBT comes in. There is a concept of being in the moment. It is a great part of what training is. So how do we get in the moment when we are being impulsive?

It can be difficult, to say the least. Impulsive, risk-taking behavior is in the moment, at the moment. Ideally, we can have a moment within the moment. A pause button before we act. When we take the time to consider someone other than ourselves in a nonjudgmental way, we can make better choices.

Better choices are not easily found when lost in a moment of impulse. DBT has a few skills for this, one is emotional or thought shock. Hot showers, cold sinks, breathwork, or even distraction by another event can give the time to examine whether things are impulsive, or a basic need, want, or expression.

Through this evaluation, the individual has the opportunity to not act impulsively and see if this is a reoccurring event. Impulse has importance. It does when our lives are in danger. Those who cannot distinguish between life and death need to take a moment and not react to every situation like they are going to die. The need is for the emotion or the thought process leading to the impulse to be temporarily broken so that something else can take its place.

There many different forms of impulsive, risk-taking, self-harming behaviors. They can be sexual, as in jumping into sexual experiences on a whim, they can be shopping/spending money impulses, they can be angry or combative emotional impulses, binge eating… the list goes on. Even over apologizing can be a form of impulsivity.

We're not talking about giving into a little temptation now and again. We all do that, and most of the time, it is not harmful to ourselves or others. Often in the case of people with BPD, impulsivity starts with tension that continues building. The cause of the tension is often an emotional trigger of some sort, and we may not even realize where it originated until we sit and examine it. The tension builds suspense and anticipation. This can happen over days, or it can happen in a matter of moments.

The impulsive act is only a culmination of that anticipation to release or relieve what we are feeling. It is an acting out against what we are feeling or perceiving, and we are not usually in control. Most often, after the impulse has been acted upon, we feel guilt or regret after. We need to break this cycle and stop the impulse before we act upon it, to stop the cycle of emotions and regret.

Therapy is the best option to help you get things under control and back on track in your life in a healthy way. DBT teaches us mindfulness. Being present in the now, in the moment, allows us to recognize when things start to feel pressing. We can stop and examine them before they get to a state that is out of control. We can identify what the cause is and start working with ourselves through breathing and refocusing to rid ourselves of unhealthy impulses. Then we can further examine the behavior when we are not in the moment of crisis.

If impulsivity or risk-taking are consistent issues, there are a few tricks we can use to prevent the possibility of future impulsive behaviors, helping us to take the beat needed to reach a place of mindfulness. Here are some options that may help. Each one is designed to make you stop and think, to reach a place of mindfulness before jumping into behaviors that may be harmful to yourself or others. Some of them are very simple, and may even seem silly, and yet they can be very effective tools to put you into the right mindset to avoid destructive behaviors.

Spending Sprees. If you feel that need to spend the money, try a couple of things… Don't bring your credit cards or bank cards with you when you head out the door. That way, when you feel the need to spend, you actually have to think about it before you have ready access to your funds. Try implementing a 24-hour rule for spending, if you absolutely have to have your cards or cash with you. Don't allow yourself to spend over $10-$20 without first waiting a 24-hour period. Or, allow yourself a specific amount of money, like $20 to spend on impulse buys per paycheck. Again, it gives you time to actually think about what you are spending your money on and why.

Anger/Emotional Outbursts. This is hard, because emotions are instinctive, and are a hard impulse not to act on. Try to be aware of your emotional state at all times. When you feel anger, outraged, or combative, try to stop and think. What is making me feel this way? How can I stop myself from feeling this way? Do I really need to say this right here, right now? If possible, try sitting on your hands. We often use the movement of our hands to emphasize our words, especially when filled with emotion. By sitting on our hands when we start to feel negative emotions rise, we give ourselves that one single extra moment to stop and think about what is happening, putting ourselves in a place of mindfulness.

As previously noted, most of this advice is simple about being mindful or finding ways to examine what you're doing instead of just jumping into it. If all else fails, walk away from the temptation, take a hot shower, breathe deeply, or even stick your head in a sink full of cold water to shock the impulse drive out of you, and then sit back and examine it again for what it might actually be… harmful to a healthy you.

Self-Harm

Unfortunately, this is the ultimate expression of the impulse of destruction. As unfortunate as this is, it is also understandable. We can harm ourselves at any moment of any day. We are indeed trapped inside of ourselves and cannot truly escape. When we do not like ourselves, we sometimes express it with self-violence.

The ultimate self-violence is to end life. This is common among those with BPD. It is the control that no one but the user has the switch too. On or off, it is up to the individual to decide.

If you do not like yourself, why not harm yourself?

This is a true statement of opinion, and opinions and feelings are valid. It is not a WISE statement.

When dealing with life and death, DBT has a concept called a wise mind.

This is the combination of emotion and logic and that there is a balance between the two.

Those who harm themselves, usually have one extreme or another that takes them over the edge. Too much emotion. Too much logic. Perhaps too much of both.

Wise mind pulls us back to a center. With the examination of both extreme logic and extreme emotion, we find that extreme may not really be what is happening. Eventually, there is wisdom only in the continuance of life. There is only wisdom in healing ourselves versus harming ourselves.

When the wise mind begins to speak and it is not true, DBT tells us to stop what we are doing until the wise mind *does* ring true.

One whose mind is disturbed will not always know what the wise mind is saying. We have to wait until we are not disturbed to hear its wisdom.

It takes months to be able to sit still while disturbed. Practice and training. Talking and practice. This is not to be used to save life on a whim.

Power and strength are not found in quitting. Power and strength are not found in holding back emotion or logic. Power and strength are found when we realize that we are out of control and need to hold our actions until we are back in control. It is the moment and the recognition of the moment that is true power. True control.

Acting out of instinct because it feels good, or will stop the pain, is not always in our best interest. Everyone falls now and again. Some more than others and this is acceptable. Repetition of control to see if something works, can only be accomplished if we live to see and try another day.

Try the 24-hour rule that was mentioned earlier when trying to stop impulsive behaviors. After all, self-harm or suicide is more often than not an act of impulse. If you feel the need to self-harm, start the clock. Allow yourself 24 hours to examine the thought and see whether or not you still find it to be a valid solution. Talk to someone. Talk to your partner or a friend, or even your therapist. They are here to help you.

The most important thing is to eventually get help. If you are having these kinds of thoughts, you are likely feeling either emotionally off-center or emotionally numb. Either way, there is help to be found. A psychiatric hold is usually 48-72 hours when they feel that someone is out to harm themselves. You are very much worth giving yourself at least 24 hours to examine what is making you feel as though there is no hope. There is always hope. Give yourself time. Be mindful. Be positive.

Extreme Emotional Swings

One moment we are sad. The next happy. How is this possible? Do we have any control over our emotions at all?

Those who have extreme emotional swings are not dysfunctional. They are just misinformed.

Everyone and that means *everyone*, goes from emotion to emotion. The speed in which we switch from one to another is up to the individual. There is no real counter as to how fast or how slow we can go from feeling to feeling. Everyone is unique.

It is in this uniqueness that we find those diagnosed with BPD are labeled with extreme emotional swings.

Extreme emotions happen. How we react to those emotions is completely a different matter.

DBT steps in again and tells us to justify our emotions at this point. In other words, before we act on extreme emotion, we need to look at it. Examination of the situation and then examining how it is being reacted to can give an indication of inappropriate extremes. At the moment where we see that there is an inappropriate extreme, we can put in another emotion, or dial back the one we are experiencing.

When an individual is lost in extreme emotion, an examination of what is happening at the moment, in a non-judgmental way, can determine appropriate action. This appropriate action and how to implement it is covered in a large section of DBT training.

However, in the high-speed world we promised, there is something that can be tried in the moment of extreme emotion…

The non-judgmental examination of self. For example, It is ok for emotions to be extreme. It is even ok that extreme emotions can be misplaced. It is better to avoid the extreme emotions that sometimes harm others. We need the harming of ourselves and others to stop. We need to realize that our emotions are harming ourselves and others. We also need to not judge ourselves for having these emotions. They happen. The world happens. We react to it. We need to find better ways to react emotionally.

It is in looking at the emotion as it is happening that we can begin to heal. Emotions happen. The trick is to examine what those emotions are… while they are happening. Not to judge them. We just need to see what they are and what causes them to happen.

After examination, we can determine if the time fits the crime. In other words, are the extreme emotions habitually self-caused, or are they appropriate to the situation at hand? If not, then we need to switch them out with another emotion or lessen the impact of how we allow the emotion to affect us.

As always, DBT teaches us mindfulness. Be in the moment, in the now with our emotions. When we can take that single breath that leads to the single thought that we are experiencing emotional extremes, we can stop. We can pause for a moment while that thought sinks in.

Anger is the most common. We exhibit and feel anger as a result of many other emotions. Anger is most often the easiest way to express our frustrations, our feelings of worthlessness or inadequacy, our feelings of disappointment. Anger flashes easily and hard. In the space between words flying out, when you have to take a breath, consciously focus on that breath. Make it a deep one. Stop before speaking again. Pause your thoughts. Hold up your hand to call a time out from the one with whom you are arguing.

Why are you angry? What exactly is it that you are feeling? Is this the real emotion, or is it covering something else, another emotion that you cannot express in words? Think about what is happening at that moment, and the what you are feeling, and how you came to this point of feeling this way.

Be mindful. Pause. Take a deep breath. Now stretch, breathe deeply, and try again.

If it is still too hard, take a break because you can't bring your emotions into focus at that moment. Try listening to some music. Change the emotion that you don't want to be experiencing, into something that you do. You are in control. You can manage your life and your emotions. You can make this happen and you are truly the only one who can do it.

Chronic Feelings of Emptiness

One of the extreme feelings or emotions for those with BPD is a feeling of emptiness. Let us be honest, everyone feels a little empty now and again.

Those working on BPD experience it in a way that is different from the rest.

Once again, this is acceptable. Being different is just that, different. We all want to be accepted and liked. It is in our nature to be part of the tribe. Those who lack a sense of self, or have trouble controlling extreme emotion, or are harming themselves directly or indirectly, are going to feel emptier than those who are not experiencing those symptoms.

Just remember you are not alone. There are others who experience the same emptiness and keep going. Your feeling of emptiness is valid. There are skills that can be put in place to help you feel less empty or to feel empty less often.

When you feel empty, first try replacing it with something else. Do something that is fun for you. Watch a comedy (try to watch something that makes you laugh versus something that scares you). Listen to music (of a happier, upbeat variety). Get lost in one of your favorite hobbies. Perhaps this could be playing a video game, making music or drawing.

The idea behind this is that when you are feeling empty, there can be a sort of "lost" feeling. It can be hard to focus on doing complex tasks. Focus your activity level on simple tasks that take little thought.

If you can't think of something you find enjoyment in, then find something to occupy you, and get your body moving. Try washing dishes. Such a task may seem small, but at the end, there is also a feeling of accomplishment. Taking a shower, sweeping or vacuuming… these are all small tasks that require little thought but get your body moving. Once your body starts moving, your thoughts will follow. This works to distract yourself from those feelings of emptiness.

This "replacing" or doing something when you feel empty will only partially fill it. This is indeed the start. A partial fill is better than no fill at all.

It takes discipline to recognize that one is empty and takes some action to do something to fill it. Here is a philosophy that may need to be considered. Others will not fill our feeling of being empty. Only we can do that. Of course, it is more fun to do it with others, however, we are ultimately the ones who must do it.

You cannot pour from an empty cup. You have nothing to give.

Only by taking the time to replenish ourselves, a little self-care, can we fill our own cup and give the others the overflow when we have it.

When we get into a routine of doing things when we feel empty, after many repetitions, we can begin to look at why we are empty. Remember that these things take time. Months of working on action to replace the feeling of emptiness is paramount before we look at the why. We need to examine some of the thoughts we may be having.

"I have a good job, why do I feel unfulfilled?"

"I know that my partner loves me, so why do I feel numb?"

"There is so much to do, and yet I just can't seem to find the energy to do anything at all."

Once we know why we are empty, it will take work to find our way back to full. The goal of being full is not easy or simple. But it starts with self-care. It starts with the realization that you are empty in the first place. It starts with changing your emotions to a more enjoyable space, whether of pleasure or accomplishment.

When we get to the why we are empty, we must break each why down into smaller and smaller and smaller parts until we can get them into bite-size chunks. Only then can we work. We must understand that it is a one step at a time and a slow, slow process to get to full. There will be failures. Impatience. Concern. Sadness. And wins.

When dealing with fixing the feeling of being empty, every small win needs to be treated as it is the most amazing thing in the world. Celebrate the wins that you have, no matter how small. Start to fill your cup little by little. Look back on the section in Chapter 2 on Taking Care of Yourself and Your Body, and the recommendations here in this chapter, and win yourself back to being full again.

Anxiousness

Extreme mental distress is a common occurrence when the personality is in question. It almost becomes a state of being. It is the jitters that keep us from taking action. It is paralyzing and downright full of fear.

Yet it is a cornerstone symptom of BPD.

And many other mental disorders.

It is believed that anxiety is in all of us. It is that part of ourselves from a long time ago when we needed to react instantly to save our lives. It is still existing within us, yet now we live in a world that does not threaten our lives every moment of every day.

We anxiously wait for something awful to happen.

How do we stop this?

We have to realize that we are not in life or death situations.

In DBT, there is radical acceptance and emotion substitution. This concept believes that similar emotions can be replaced with other emotions. And we can look at the Olympics to see an example of this.

Olympic athletes get nervous right? The pressure, the stress, anxiety is everywhere. When we look at interviews with Olympic athletes, we begin to see a pattern in their speech. The word nervous or anxious is replaced with excitement.

They are excited to be at the starting line. They are excited to feel the pressure to make that dive perfect. They are excited to feel the pressure.

This is the ultimate emotion exchange. Excitement gives the body the same reaction as anxiety does. Same feelings, same chemical reaction, same charge. Yet when we consider that excitement is not as harmful to us as anxiousness, the substitution for one for the other becomes very wise.

When you start to feel anxious, try replacing that emotion with one of excitement, or one of certainty. Emotional replacement is a key element to get past the most negative emotions. Just like when we are depressed, listening to upbeat music can change the negative emotion for one that is more positive.

If replacing anxiety with trying to feel excited, certain, or confident is not working for you, try calming music or calm breathing techniques. Calm your emotions. Take a look at them. Are you looking at the clock and it reads 7 pm, and you know your date will be over at 8 pm, are you really feeling anxious? Or is it that you are feeling fear that you will soon be alone again, abandoned? This can lead to anxiety, but anxiety is not the emotion itself that is being triggered. What is the emotion you are feeling beneath the anxiety?

There are some techniques, situation-dependent, that you can use to help stave off these feelings of anxiety. Mindfulness is the best technique overall, but when we are in a place of being anxious, that can sometimes be hard to accomplish. Being in the now, turning your focus to what is really happening is the best way to fight through your anxiety.

Set a Time. When you start to feel anxious, and you are not in a place to be mindful in the moment, take a deep breath. Calm yourself and set a time in your head to focus on what your anxiety is really about. This allows your conscious brain to stop and say, "Hey… I'm not forgetting that I'm anxious, and I am going to find out what is really going on, but for the moment, I have to just be where I am. When you finally do take that time to examine what is going on, examine everything from a place of perspective outside yourself.

Write it Down. When you are feeling particularly anxious, write the anxiety down and put it somewhere safe, in a place all their own. Know that they are there. It helps to acknowledge that you are having anxiety, but it doesn't mean you have to address it in the immediate moment. Know that you will take a moment for yourself at a later point, to examine all of your anxieties for the root cause. Maybe you will find a pattern that you can further examine to break free of your anxiety cycle and move into a healthier space of mind and emotion.

Shift Your Focus. If you are not in a place to stop everything and examine your levels of anxiety, then shift your focus to something else. Try just focusing on the place where you are at right now, you can either write these things down or mentally tick them off in your head. What time is it? What is the ambiance like? What is the temperature? What day is it? Indoors or outdoors? What kind of furniture is in the room? What kind of cars are going by? Force yourself to look at every little thing and detail. Give yourself something else to focus on, other than your anxiety.

Talk to Someone. Maybe you are comfortable enough with your date to talk with them about you feeling a little anxious. Maybe you are not in that place yet. Oversharing with someone who is not familiar enough with you may not be the best solution to recovering from your anxiety in the moment. But talking to someone else, a friend, loved one, or your therapist can be extremely helpful in calming and examining where your anxiety might be coming from.

Breathe. Breathe deeply. Breathe again. Breathing and mindful focus on our breathing is one of the simplest ways to calm anxiety, and yet it is also the most easily forgotten when we are in the middle of feeling anxious. Work with breathing when you are not feeling anxious. Make it a regular part of who you are… calm, collected, and emotionally healthy.

Depression

Those dealing with BPD will have more downtime than up. This means that overall, the experience of more negative emotions feeds the loss—the loss of connection, the loss of feeling (like when we are empty), etc. It is easier to maintain sadness or fear rather than happiness or hope. We tend to lean toward what is easier.

One strength of DBT is to recognize that we have emotions. We have these emotions for a reason. It used to be for protection. The hairs on the back of your neck rising once was recognized as a sign that you are being hunted. That is normally still true.

Depression tells us that something is not working.

We need to first recognize that depression is natural. It is ok to be depressed. It is not right or wrong. We do not point fingers at ourselves and say depression. It is just a feeling, and it is trying to tell you something.

However, in the moment of depression, it is super difficult to examine anything. When all you want to do is crawl into the closet for days, an examination of why the emotion is happening is not on the top of the survival list.

Depression is a feeling. Feelings tell us something is happening that we are not processing in a logical way. They are a wakeup call. Normally, our emotions and feelings are a wakeup call to take action.

Are we sad? Let's take action to fix being sad. Are we happy? Oh… let's repeat this so that we can feel this again! And so on.

Depression usually tells us that something harmful has happened, emotionally or otherwise. It is also possible that we are not taking action to get us what we want. This symptom of BPD is one of a spiral.

We feel depressed. We know we have not taken action. We feel MORE depressed. We remember that we have still not taken action. We feel even more depressed.

This cycle can be broken with small successes, one after another.

DBT focuses on examination (logical mind) of emotions (emotional mind) and shows us that a nice, non-judgmental view of what is happening yields wisdom. In this wisdom, there is normally action. This action needs to be encouraged no matter how small, or whether it is even successful. Keep trying until success is achieved, and at the same time, praise yourself for your efforts.

Depression can be beaten back with laughter. Until you understand why you are depressed, try some techniques to produce laughter, happiness, or simple enjoyment. Depression and your feelings may be yelling at you to have some fun. So have your fun, and work later.

This is the opposite action that gives relief to see what is actually causing the depression.

It is immensely difficult to work on depression while depressed. Give yourself a break. Many, if you need to. And no judging, or beating yourself up.

Remember, emotions are there for a reason. Mindfulness techniques we have been bringing into this time and time again are an important way to deal with emotions, and they work very well when trying to deal with depression. Here are a few techniques that can either help fight the depression, change it, or bring yourself to a mindful place to examine it for what it is and where it is coming from.

Listen to Music. This has been said already but fits well here. If you find yourself depressed, try doing something to change your mood, such as listening to upbeat, uplifting, or happy music, curl up in a blanket and watch a comedy or your favorite (non-depressing) television show, snuggle with your favorite stuffed toy, or cuddle with your pet. All of these things trigger endorphins that can help move you from a place of depression.

Write. Try writing your negative feelings, or reasons to be depressed on a piece of paper. It helps to identify them and get them out, putting you in a better place to examine them from a place of mindfulness. Are you done checking them all out? Good. Now burn them in a fire-safe bowl or the sink, or just simply tear them up and throw them away. Try to turn your focus toward something other than the depression, now that you have identified why it is there.

Goal Setting. Not all cases, but often when we are depressed it can be linked to the past. Goal setting is a great way to start focusing on the future and working towards a more desirable life/outcome. Something that will fulfill us or makes us feel extremely proud if we are achieved it, is great to work towards. Goal setting can also be therapeutic, allowing us to envision a bright future focusing on positivity. When writing down your goals, break it down into short-term goals and long-term goals as this will make it easier to achieve and help you feel progression.

If that didn't do the trick, then try writing a comforting letter to the depressed side of yourself. Tell yourself all of the reasons why you shouldn't be feeling depressed, examine the positives and check them away with each thing you tell yourself, just as you would a dear friend who came to you in their time of depression. This time, that dear friend is you. What do you need to tell yourself that might help you to feel better?

The best way to overcome our emotions is to be aware of them, mindful in the moment. Work with those things that can help you get to a place where you can apply logic and focus to your emotions and deal with them one at a time, one step at a time.

Hostility

Hostility is the outcome of fear. Aggression is founded in fear.

Hostile behavior is a cornerstone of BPD. It is best described from a tribal point of view. Ever since mankind started to form tribes, there has been a standing hostility from tribe to tribe. This is the reaction of one family to another.

Needless to say, we have been hostile for a long, *long* time.

Some of the symptoms and conditions of hostility are outbursts and lashing out of the physical. Everything from passive-aggressive silent violence to the screaming of someone who has lost their mind.

Those who fear abandonment can be hostile. Those who have problems determining their sense of self tend to have short fuses. When we are anxious, we can turn to hostility, not realizing that the hostility may actually cause the same situation we are anxious to avoid.

Those who are suffering and are in pain have difficulty explaining that pain to others while it is happening. It leads to hostility. This can cause us to lash out. Most of the time, the one being hostile is doing it out of habit.

This is where we are going to address DBT and get those skills rolling. It is in the hostility that we have the most difficulty discerning what is life-threatening and what is not. It makes sense that the ancient tribal feeling of being hostile indicated that their life was feeling threatened.

It is in this moment that those suffering lose control.

That is what we want. That is what DBT wants. Individuals retaining some semblance of control. Here is why.

When we scream and rant and harm, we get a result. It is not necessarily the result we want. This is better than no result at all, correct?

That is uncertain. Thinking about what is healthy and not, we begin to see that a reaction equal to feeling your life being threatened, when it is just a plate broken in the kitchen, is not healthy. This is the difference in survival and perpetual suffering.

We cause ourselves to suffer. Hostility on a constant scale is a form of suffering. Unstoppable and always happening is not how the human condition is set up. We must find a way to examine ourselves while it is happening so that we can remain safe and not harm ourselves or others.

Almost anything hostile is harming someone or something.

So why act hostile if it harms us?

Sometimes we have to fight. To ignore this impulse completely is an incomplete set of emotions. Hostility has its place.

DBT tells us that we need to look at WHY we are feeling hostility. It is possible that the mind cannot process what is going on and shuts down. During this shutdown, the individual sees that there are all these emotions taking place. When we pick hostility, we get the body active again. This feeling of hostility is telling us to take action.

It does not necessarily mean violent action. In fact, it may be telling us to make a change in our lives so that hostility subsides.

Try watching for signs of anger and hostility. These signs are the same as date back to our tribal ancestors and back to our basic survival instincts of fight or flight. Your heart starts beating faster. Your breathing quickens. You start tapping your feet. Your body tenses up, and you start clenching your jaw or your fists. Be mindful at all times, aware of where you are at and what you are feeling.

Try some simple techniques to calm your anger. Breathe deeply and slowly. Count to ten. Try relaxing your body, unclenching your fists or jaw. Be mindful of how you are feeling, and what is causing you to feel this way. Remove yourself from the situation and go for a walk.

If that doesn't get you to a place where you are more in control of your emotions, try expressing your emotions in a different, less harmful way… Try tearing up a newspaper into little bits, hitting a pillow or other soft surface that won't cause you damage, maybe chuck ice cubes into the sink or tub to shatter them. These are all less harmful ways of allowing for emotional expression without hurting yourself or others.

If none of this works, try distraction techniques. Work on something with your hands, making or fixing something. Try taking a cold shower, shocking your system into thinking about something else. Maybe coloring, drawing, or journaling is more your style. Exercise can move us into a better place of mindful awareness. Whatever it takes to bring you from that emotion into a mental and emotional space where you can better examine what is going on is where your focus needs to be.

We are built to have emotions, after all. We just need to apply a healthy emotion to our situations, and when we see an emotion that is not healthy, we need to change it and see what is going on.

Chapter 10: Skills for the Other Side of the Relationship

Loving and being in a relationship with someone who is struggling with Borderline Personality Disorder is not easy. It is hard to go from being under emotional attack to being a supportive partner. It is with your understanding and willingness to work with those you love that you can help to bring them to a healthier emotional and mental place for you both.

How do we help those who are suffering?

This chapter is going to touch on all the symptoms we discussed in the last chapter and we are going to give a little suggestion to those who live alongside someone with BPD.

First off, you cannot change anyone.

They can only change themselves.

You can, however, create an environment so that they can grow and be the person they want to be. It is said with certainty that those suffering BPD do not like who they are and want to be something more than what they currently are.

This is where you can shine. Creating an environment that is healthy, creative and understanding can make it so that the individual that you snuggle up to can get the help they need.

Here is the second fact.

They need to ask for help.

Yes, you as the other person *must* wait for them to ask for help. To diagnose them and then start applying treatment will do nothing for a BPD individual but pour gasoline on an already lit bonfire.

The duty of those trying to help those suffering symptoms of BPD is to not press. It is to offer. Continuously offer.

Third.

Your health is on the table as well.

When the situation is too unhealthy, you have every right to express yourself. Those who lack a sense of self and are living in fear need to hear that they are not the only one hurting. There is always the bonus that when you help someone else, you, in turn, get more than they do.

That is the nature of helping. It is super difficult to ask for help. Sometimes help is needed to even ask for help. In the end, the teacher becomes the student and those helping and creating an environment for health to become healthier themselves.

It's a win-win.

Finally, before we get to the symptoms and how to deal with them, we need to talk about safety.

Safety for those suffering is paramount. This includes both sides of the relationship. When we feel unsafe, we need to speak up. When our voices are unheard when it concerns our safety, we need to consider backing away.

It is completely ok to back away from an unsafe situation. This is not an uncaring act. This is acceptable health.

And now, the flip side of that which we already discussed.

Fear of Abandonment, or the Terror of Being Left Alone.

From the perspective of those living with a partner who constantly fears abandonment, there are a few actions they can take. One is to create an environment that we discussed above. The individual with BPD needs room to grow without feeling like they are abandoned, or about to be abandoned.

Communication is key here. Telling them why and where you are. Being straight helps as well. Letting them know you are doing what you are doing for what reason, with the constant understanding that you are not judging them.

They will feel judged.

It is a factual moment. A logical moment. A helping of what they are going through.

They have fear.

You may have to give them a little hope.

When we do these things in small amounts, they are digestible. The first instinct is to throw everything into hope and slide it across the table and there it is. Remember that the person over there is suffering extremes. They need small bites. Smaller bites than what you are used to.

Small bites of hope.

Unclear or Shifting Self-Image?

Self-image is difficult to implement or help. Since it is something that we all find in ourselves, healing someone with a lack of self-identity can be very tricky indeed.

The best recommendation is to refer them to someone who is professionally trained. The sculpting of an individual's mental self is compared to extensive brain surgery.

Over months and months.

In the short run, the key to helping those who suffer from their self-image is in understanding what is happening. Those who lack a sense of self are often at the mercy of others to define that self. This is a coping tool and is not a cure. Allowing a non-judgmental view of what self is can go a long way to those without it.

There is also leading by example. Showing how your self reacts and applies to situations, explaining it as you would to a child, can help.

Remember as well that we are not talking about just lack of image, but a shifting of image. Sometimes they will not be able to control it. Patience in different situations may be required. The more you make yourself flexible, the more they will relate to you. Showing stability in your own self-identity, yet being flexible when events happen or things change will be of benefit.

Maybe when you change yourself, they will learn from it, and in return, you may like that you can change a bit.

Flexibility allows for all kinds of new opportunities.

There is a plastic surgeon by the name of Maxwell Malts who noticed that even after surgery and having amazing changes made to their bodies and faces, some of his patients still suffered from low self-esteem and a lack of clear self-image or identity. This didn't sit well with him, as he was in the business of making people feel better about themselves.

He went through years of study and research which led him to write his book on self-image: *Psycho-Cybernetics: A New Way To Get More Out Of Living Life*. It talks about self-image and how it has an impact on every aspect of your life, how changing your thought patterns and habits can actually bring change to your life, and that setbacks and failures don't have to define you, they can actually be used as progress to create successes in your life. It is a well-written book that could have a great impact and benefits for those who struggle with BPD and their partners.

Impulsive/Self-destructive Behaviors

The impulse here is what we are going to look at. It is super easy to react to those who explode. You may indeed build many great things, from relationship parts to building actual physical things.

Your sand castle will get knocked over by those with BPD.

Why?

Because they are trying to see how others react to destructive behavioral situations. This will tell them whether or not they are being too extreme. They will keep trying.

This is where one needs to take a breath and explain it like they are dealing with a child, for the emotions of someone with BPD have been harmed early in their life.

When a child harms an adult, it is up to the adult to treat the child with sternness, yet retaining the discipline addressed to a child.

What we mean by this is that you need to remember that emotionally they are still like a child.

This is not to say they are. Forgiveness does have a limit. It is in the creation of the environment for them, that it becomes safe, even with destructive behavior evident.

In showing that you are not fazed by destruction (without fear of life… if you fear for your life… be fazed) destruction will become less and less. Communicating about how the destruction affects you in a non-violent and non-judgmental way, can yield great results.

A destructive child is that way for a reason. They are unable to process the correct emotion to the situation at hand.

DBT individuals, when in a group, have a way of talking to one another. When a person cannot process what is happening to them, they cannot help themselves. When the moment arises where those suffering cannot figure out what is going on, a series of questions can be asked.

Do you know why you are being destructive?

No.

Do you want to be a destructive person?

No (if yes, then take a breath and let them calm down and ask again until you get a no).

Do you know how to be less destructive?

No.

And here is the best question of all. Never throw suggestions at someone who is suffering. They are not drowning. They are trying to redefine themselves and this line of questioning will help. Now we finish with this question.

Are you open to suggestions?

When, and only when, they say yes, are you to help them. When they say no, you are to leave them to it. They are not ready yet. Do not fret. The repetition of destructive behavior will arise again. And we can repeat the questions back to them until they say yes to suggestions.

Self-Harm

Individuals are in control of their bodies and minds. It is not up to anyone but the user to take command or sub-command of their existence.

When we are talking about an individual who harms themselves, we are talking about the very core of what we can and cannot do to ourselves.

We are talking about personal freedom. Removing freedom from anyone or anything is not really positive.

So how do we help those who are harming themselves?

By waiting.

To wait is often the most difficult thing in life. When others harm themselves, they are most likely going for attention. Or perhaps they are defining who they are. This is a very normal condition. We are talking about control at a primal level.

In this control, one can harm themselves. Even when you place them in a straitjacket, they can mash their skull on the concrete until it opens and they bleed out. The only way to truly stop someone who is self-harming is to allow them to find out themselves that they are in control and life can be worth living if they work at making it better.

Now there is the logical side of DBT that can come into play here. When we start to talk about the *why* of self-harm. When we remove the stigmas and the taboos of self-harm and just talk about it in a flat way, we begin to get to the facts of why it is happening.

On the side of those living with someone who is self-harming, the *when* of the discussion is essential.

Do not discuss facts while an individual is self-harming or attempting to self-harm.

Put your arms around them with all your loving intent, and then just listen and wait. Discuss facts the next day, or when they are more at peace. It is in the extreme that you have to not be extreme.

Speaking of extreme…

Extreme Emotional Swings

Considering the nature of emotions and that we all have them, the individual with BPD experiences emotions in a very different way. What is a normal extreme emotion to another is nothing compared to those without a sense of self and personality shifts experience.

It is in this extreme that they become lost. It is possible that after years of having extreme emotions that an individual begins to cultivate the ability to extend the extreme by flipping back and forth from one emotion to the next.

DBT proves that an average emotion only lasts about fifteen minutes.

When you are trying to handle someone who is jumping about with their emotions in an extreme way, remaining calm may indeed infuriate them.

One would think that remaining calm during this extreme outburst is the best option. There is one better. Affirmation.

When you affirm what the person is suffering it allows a connection to them. This connection during times of extreme emotional flux also allows the individual suffering to have some relief about abandonment.

Affirming what they are going through and communicating with someone who is on the extreme can yield positive results. An example of this is sadness.

When BPD individuals experience an emotion like sadness, they are not just sad. They are suicidal sad. Their tanks empty so quickly, and they are left with nothing but distress and emptiness.

It is in this moment that a touch on emotion can help. When you express your own sadness to someone who is extremely sad, they attune to the level that is not extreme. BPD individuals do not want to be drained. They just do not know how to stop it.

DBT works on emotion regulation, not removal. It also works on examples, recommendations, and someone else being a sounding board so that we do not judge our emotions.

Showing someone with extreme emotions that it only lasts so long and that they are not alone by relating to the same emotions is the start. Eventually, those not afflicted with BPD will experience the relief of the emotion. That can be communicated, very gently, to another.

"My sadness is going away, is yours?"

Always speak in questions if you can.

Chronic Feelings of Emptiness

The emotional tanks of those with BPD get drained very quickly. It is beyond just a mental state. The body suffers as well. This leaves them grouchy, irritable, and most certainly empty.

The emptiness comes also from many different feelings. Fear

makes you feel empty when it has run its course. Loneliness makes you feel empty. Anger makes you very empty after it's over.

Those who experience emotion changes, self-changes, and harm, have no choice but to feel empty.

Or do they?

It is commented in DBT that we forget to take care of the form. Emptiness can be defeated with a glass of water. Sounds like madness, right? How can an emotional outburst be beaten by a glass of water?

It is not just water. It is the caring of the body of one suffering BPD after the outburst. An aftercare, so to speak. They go through such a rigorous ordeal when outbursts happen. When there is no care after… emptiness enters.

DBT has months of training to teach us to physically self-soothe. Since we are doing high-speed DBT here, the soothing may have to come from the other person in the relationship.

When your loved one has reached that point of emptiness, they are rundown, adrenaline has run its course, and now they are just… spent. There are a few ways that you can reach out and touch them on a physical level that can help them start to replenish those feelings of emptiness and show them that you really care, regardless of what has just happened.

Massage may be a bit much at this point because their muscles are likely still overly tight from the chemical reaction of their emotional outburst in their body. A nice, gentle, soothing touch, brushing across their body can help bring them to a calmer place where they can recognize that they are loved.

Or get a nice blanket, wrap it around them and let them lean into you while sitting together on the couch. This feeling of emptiness following such an emotional outburst can create feelings akin to shock afterward, and helping to care for them at this level can be very helpful.

Replenishing their protein levels can also be beneficial at this time. So can a small treat, like chocolate or small bits of fruit. It is not about rewarding their behavior, it is about caring for them so they can replenish what they have just spent in energy.

Eventually teaching those who suffer that they are actually, physically empty, and they need to fill themselves, will be needed. For now…

A glass of water defeats emptiness, especially when it is given by someone who cares.

Anxiousness

Everyone experiences anxiety. The daily stress of life haunts us all. We have this incredible urge to jump up and take action when we need to remain still. We all have ants in our pants.

This jumpiness is magnified in those who do not regulate emotions. It is also increased when it is combined with something like fear. Without a sense of self, anxiousness becomes a full-time pre-occupation.

Those suffering from anxiety can use DBT to replace this feeling with another, healthier emotion. To do this may require some outside help.

Bringing your partner to a place of mindfulness can be very effective, but difficult to do when they are full of anxiety. A simple task to help them is to remind them to breathe. Breathe deeply. This is a simple thing that is often forgotten in the moment but can be the best tool to calm those who are in the middle of an anxiety attack.

While you are getting them to breathe, reminding those who are struggling with anxiety that they are truly not in a life or death situation may seem mundane. Of course, their life is not being threatened. To them, it very much feels as though it is.

It is in this reminder, no matter how many times we remind them, is a place where they will eventually relax enough to see what is happening inside of themselves. The only way that this stops for them is to talk to them while it is happening, help them to see that they are not facing a life or death situation, and bring them to a place where they can better identify what is truly going on inside of themselves.

Once the extremeness of the feeling is removed, you can then begin to talk about replacing anxiety with another emotion.

Depression

All the way down. Down to the very bottom. To a place where there is no escape. Make sure that the rope is severed. The ladder is crushed. We are down here and we have made it so that we cannot get back up. This is the place of those with BPD.

This is a depression that is very tricky. A hand to help them up is not necessarily what they need. A light thrown down is also not what they need. Even recognition of where they are is only going to drive them further into depression.

DBT to the rescue.

Opposite action is required here. When depression is weighing down on those suffering doing the exact opposite is the way to go… make them feel happiness, pleasure, joy.

This is where you can help. When you create an environment that is not depressing and you take those suffering there, the chance of them climbing out is more attainable.

This is not to say that they won't try to take the positive environment and turn it into a sarcastic, negative thing. We must let them have their negativity. Their negativity is what is keeping them from sinking further. Our skill is to wait that out.

When we are unaffected by those who suffer depression and continue to be positive, we teach them that there is another way to live. When they feel depressed, they have an action to take if they choose— to do something happy.

This happiness-defeating depression technique needs to be trained into those who sink into the darkness. This skill set is very difficult indeed. It is difficult to do anything while majorly depressed. Frustration and failure are easily in the way here.

Those on the other side of the relationship can help those with BPD. It is in the creating of positivity and then showing them that you won't allow them to wallow in their depression and that you can see a light. Bring them to this space. Put them in it. Do not press them while they are in it. Just let them see, and always offer inclusion. Go for a cup of coffee… or hot chocolate. Do things that you know bring them pleasure.

Remind them of their wonderful qualities and traits. Remind them what it is you love about them. Talk to them about future plans, making them feel that there is security of a future with you.

Risk-Taking

Understanding when it comes to risk-taking is like walking a tricky balance beam. It is a potential mix of harm to your loved one and harm to everyone around them.

Harm to the individual with BPD requires a soft touch. Discussing the harm to others that comes from their risk-taking can be a little sterner.

Those taking risk in order to feel or to experience and define life is essential for self-identification. It is the little child touching a hot stove and burning their hand to understand what hot is. To not touch things that are hot. They identify self this way.

Those with BPD do not have this sense of self and they take the constant risk to find themselves.

The best way to deal with this from an outside perspective is **communication**. The questions surrounding the why of risk-taking will allow the self in BPD to be defined without so much of the harm of risk.

DBT deals with risk in a very interesting way. It teaches us to pause while the risk is happening. It is a way to be non-judgmental and examine fact rather than thought. When the fact is laid out and all personal thought is removed, we begin to see exactly why risk is happening.

Risk understanding is found in the wise mind while utilizing fact-finding in the logical mind. Removing the emotion while risk-taking is acceptable behavior. It is when emotions run away that the risks we take become so dangerous.

When risk-taking harms others, a sterner approach needs to take place. Do not allow yourself or others to be harmed by the risk-taking of those with BPD. They will sometimes take risks to try to harm you to see what that does, or to test the waters.

Try to not overreact or panic if your loved one or partner is involved in taking risks. Remember, they may be trying to elicit a response from you. You can't give that to them, or you will create a pattern of behavior that they may repeat in the future. You want to talk with them about their risk-taking in a calm, non-judgmental way, in order to get them to reach into their wise mind and determine why they are taking such risks in the first place.

Being calm and explaining to them that you are not to be harmed by their risk-taking is necessary. You need to set clear boundaries and hold them accountable to keeping them. Relate to them as the person that they are, not just their behaviors. Try open and honest communication. Let them know your fears as to what they are doing, and how you feel it harms you. Do it in a calm manner, and let them help you understand the reasons behind their actions, or offer to help them think through their reasons.

If the behavior continues, there are only a few alternatives for you to take. Find a professional to help.

And if none of that works? Do not remain in a harmful situation. Walk away from those who take constant, destructive risks that harm you and others.

Hostility

There comes a time where a line has to be drawn. Hostility is not to be tolerated. People who struggle with BPD can lash out with anger and hostility whenever you do not do what they want or expect. You didn't come home on time from work? They don't understand that your boss kept you late. They only understand that you are.

In their mind, you have gone from loving partner to someone who is hurting them by not keeping their promises. There is rarely a middle ground with someone who suffers from BPD. In their eyes, a situation or a person is either black or white, grey is a color, not a situational option. They will often yell, make threats or accusations, scream… their behaviors are often way out of proportion to whatever the situation actually is.

Just trying to understand that it happens can lead to allowing it to happen more than once. The wise mind found in DBT skill sets can determine whether hostility is justified or not.

The wise mind is where the rational, thinking mind overlaps with the emotional, reactive mind. It is the place where mindfulness takes root and helps us to understand what is happening, how it is manifesting, and eventually, why we reached that place.

When we stop to examine whether the hostility is justified, more often than not, it is not.

It is important to be supportive of your loved one or partner, but support for those who are hostile is only effective if all parties are safe.

Chapter 11: Mindfulness

Mindfulness in DBT is actively practiced during the nine- to twelve-month program. Mindfulness is the core of the wise mind applied. As we said in the previous chapter, the wise mind is where the rational and emotional minds overlap and meet in understanding. Mindfulness is how we get there.

Mindfulness is core to the practice of almost all DBT techniques and skills. Those who deal with BPD live almost always in their emotions. There is no balance with the rational mind, therefore, there is no real understanding of what is happening emotionally.

Mindfulness teaches us to take a breath, take that moment, look at *what* is happening in the now, and *how* we are dealing with it. Mindfulness is used any time we get overly emotional, any time we lack an understanding of what is going on with ourselves or others. It is our ability to be able to reach a place of understanding so that we can act, instead of react.

It is a technique that should be practiced daily, even when not in distress so that we can more easily find that place of mindfulness when the extremity of our emotions hits us. It is the best tool for us to use in living a healthier life and bringing that emotional health into our relationships.

DBT has multiple ways to describe mindfulness. We are going to break it down into two question words.

What? and How?

Notice how we are not asking why. Why comes later. Mindfulness starts with the examination of *what* is happening in the now and *how* it is being manifested.

Some practices can be simplified.

The *what* of mindfulness is broken down into three states of mind. Observation, Description, and Participation.

The *what* of *observation* is the simplification of stopping everything and noticing what you are sensing. It is in this examination of the senses that we begin to notice what the experience is. The centering of the mind and controlling attention allows us to be alert to every thought.

When we observe, we must do it from a purely outside standpoint. If we have thoughts attached to what we are observing, we must let go of the thought, so as not to let it judge what we are experiencing one way or another. The moving of idea and thought out of our mind is essential to understanding what is actually happening. We can allow honor and respect for what we may have noticed.

Then we release it.

This allows for pure observation of what is happening.

Now we can begin to *describe* the *what* aspect of our question. Sometimes these words are not directly related to the event taking place. Like a stomach ache trying to describe sadness. Words are what describe the experience. When left to just thinking about the experience, a slippery slope begins and those suffering can slide into the darkness of overthinking and circular logic.

Simple labels and words, that may at the time feel unconnected, are the way to discern thought from actual experiences. This is mindfulness, the control of thought and the description of the actual.

This is just the facts. The *why* you are sad is not here. The gut-wrenching effect behind sadness is a plain fact. Simple. When described out loud with a word, it is direct observation.

Pure mindfulness.

The *what* of *participation* is very difficult indeed.

We are looking at present experiences versus past experiences. The mind sometimes cannot discern the difference from what *has* happened to us as opposed to what *is* happening to us. It is the letting go of the rumination.

How we do this is to become one with what we are doing. In this, there is a mindfulness that allows you to forget yourself and lose yourself in the moment. It is not letting the past affect you and participating in the now.

This is a very intuitive process. The wise mind can sometimes be a gut reaction to what is happening around us. It is in the direct participation, the going with the flow so to speak, that we do just the things that are needed for that situation alone.

The mindfulness of participation is one of intuitive action focusing not on the self and past, but rather on the moment and the passion in it. An example of this is when we color. Coloring like a child with crayon or pen or paint allows us to attempt to participate in the now. It is just about drawing.

As was said before, mindfulness should be practiced regularly, even when not in distress. In this way you can find mindfulness more easily and quickly when you do need it. It needs to become a part of your lifestyle, a tool that you carry with you always and practice with often.

Pick a topic, any topic. Maybe something that irritates you a little. Observe it from your outside point of view. Don't let yourself focus on any particular thought about it, just calm your mind and look at it.

Now allow yourself to describe what that irritation is. Use simple words, simple descriptions. Don't focus on complex thoughts or equations here. We are trying to be non-judgmental, not trying to nitpick the concept apart.

From here we slip into participation. Don't focus on past incidents, focus on the here and now. How is this affecting you in the now, not in the past? Examine what comes to mind and realize that it is a singular incident, not a continually connected, non-ending torment that we experience every day. We are only looking at the now. What is affecting me with this situation, and how is it affecting me *now*?

That skill placed in mindfulness can allow us to deal with something in the extreme, like self-harm.

The *how* of mindfulness is broken down into three skills as well. Non-judgmental, One-minded, and Effectiveness.

When we remove judgment of ourselves, we can breathe.

Examination of the *how* of the facts gives us space to *stop judging* ourselves.

This can be accomplished by removing evaluation. We are not to determine whether emotions or actions are good or bad. We are looking at just the facts. One way to do this is to remove opinions. When we stop allowing ourselves to have an opinion about how something is happening, we can just relax and let it happen. Opinions are valid, yet not always needed. In the case of mindfulness, opinions are not needed.

This allows for open acceptance of each moment. We can see and acknowledge the helpful, the wholesome, and yet not judge it.

There are times when trying to implement non-judgmental behavior when it is all too easy to judge your judging. Judging yourself for judging is not mindfulness. It is the opposite. We all judge ourselves. It is time to stop doing that.

With the *one-minded* aspect of the *how*, we are being completely present in the moment. We do not go somewhere else in our minds. We remain completely focused and working on one thing at a time.

When you are eating, eat. When you are working, work. When you are remembering something, just remember. When you are breathing deep to find your calm, breathe deep. Do each thing with all your attention and focus.

This is the letting go of distraction. In our modern world, we are completely surrounded by distractions. Mindfulness is all about letting go of these distractions. This is very difficult indeed.

Mindfulness requires concentration and focus. When we try to do two things at once, we must go back and forth from one to another. It is scientifically proven the mind does only one thing at a time. Multi-tasking is a society-created myth. Regardless of scientific proof, one thing at a time is the way of pure mindfulness.

Mindfulness in the *how* is about *effectiveness*. When we focus on one thing at a time, we begin to focus on what works. This is the utilization of the skills at the moment. It is not about wishing that we are in a different situation while we are still in the one that we are in. Mindfulness of the *how* is in the skillful application of the now.

This is the eye of the tiger. The keeping of your objectives in mind and doing everything necessary to achieve a goal. In this, we are doing just what is needed actively, not passively. Sitting on our hands is not acceptable mindfulness.

This mindfulness of the how allows us to change harmful behaviors. Both situations and our reactions to them can be accepted as what they are versus what we *think* they are.

The most important part of mindfulness is letting go.

When we let go of vengeance, anger and the righteousness of our hurt, we get to what works.

Conclusion

Dealing with Borderline Personality Disorder is not easy, but steps can be taken, skills built, tools sharpened, and the work put in to make life so much better than how it may be seen and experienced in the now.

DBT is a very beneficial tool that helps to build these skill sets needed to have a happy life with or without a partner. Just in picking up this book, you have shown the willingness and interest in taking the first step toward a better future for yourself and your loved ones.

A last note on mindfulness… Mindfulness can be achieved through a variety of techniques and is a strong component of Dialectical Behavioral Therapy. It is the tool used to punctuate all of the other tools and skills that you are taught in therapy.

One way to bring the strength of mindfulness into your life is to practice through meditation.

Other highly recommended resources to help you on your journey include:

- *True Buddhism: A Beginners Guide to Transforming Suffering, Chaos and Rage into Peace, Joy and Enlightenment through the Teachings and Philosophy of Buddha – Includes Guided Meditation.*

Many of the techniques found in those pages can be directly correlated to the techniques utilized in DBT, especially when it comes to learning mindfulness.

- *Guided Meditation for Insomnia, Anxiety and Stress Relief: Heal Yourself with Deep Hypnosis Relaxation, Learn to Let Go, and Get a Great Night's Sleep*

This is a great guided meditation audiobook with beautiful background music. It will help you to relax your mind and practice mindfulness. Give it a try.

This brings us to the end. I hope you have found this book helpful for you and your relationship and are able to apply the information learned in this book. I commend you for taking the steps to a better life and facing your demons. You are on the right track.

Please let me know what was your favorite part of the book and what you found most helpful, in the form of a review. Not only does it bring me great joy to know I have helped people in need, but it will also help others searching for help with their BPD and relationship.

Thank you